The ART of SPELLING

ALSO BY MARILYN VOS SAVANT

The ART of SPELLING

The Madness and the Method

MARILYN VOS SAVANT

Illustrations by Joan Reilly

W. W. NORTON & COMPANY
New York · London

Copyright © 2000 by Marilyn vos Savant

All rights reserved
Printed in the United States of America
First Edition

For information about permission to reproduce
selections from this book, write to Permissions,
W. W. Norton & Company, Inc., 500 Fifth Avenue,
New York, NY 10110

The text and display of this book are composed in
Stone Serif.
Composition by Thomas Ernst
Manufacturing by Quebecor World, Fairfield
Book design by Charlotte Staub

Library of Congress Cataloging-in-Publication Data

Vos Savant, Marilyn, date.
        The art of spelling : the madness and the
    method / by Marilyn vos Savant ; illustrations by
    Joan Reilly.
        p.   cm.
    Includes bibliographical references and index.
    ISBN 0-393-04903-5
    1. English language—Orthography and spelling.
        I. Title.

PE1143.V67 2000
421'52—dc21   00-037228

W. W. Norton & Company, Inc., 500 Fifth Avenue,
New York, N.Y. 10110
www.wwnorton.com

W. W. Norton & Company Ltd., 10 Coptic Street,
London WC1A 1PU

1 2 3 4 5 6 7 8 9 0

Dedicated to my dear husband,
Rob Jarvik, who is utterly brilliant
in every other way, but whose
spelling could use a teensy
bit of improvement.

ACKNOWLEDGMENT

I want to thank my assistant Joan Reilly, without whose excellent judgment and fine research skills this book would not have been possible. Joan managed to assemble the entire project from scratch, flagging only when she was asked to find out whether Queen Elizabeth I (1558–1603) was a good speller.

CONTENTS

The ART of SPELLING

FOREWORD

Man Sues Over Misspelled Tattoo
Thursday, February 25, 1999
Roseville, MI (AP)

A man who used guesswork instead of a dictionary when getting a tattoo is now suing the tattoo parlor over the mistaken spelling of *villain*. Lee Williams was left with "villian" on his right forearm, but he didn't notice until a friend made fun of him, according to the Circuit Court lawsuit filed Wednesday. Williams, 23, is seeking $25,000 in damages against Eternal Tattoos. To cover up the mistake he had plastic surgery, which cost him $1,900 and left a "scar as long as his forearm," said his lawyer, Paul Clark. Williams, a student at Wayne State University and a former Marine, got the tattoo in 1996. Before the procedure, workers at the parlor debated how to spell the word, Clark said. Williams wasn't sure, either, and they settled on "villian," Clark said. Eternal Tattoos' owner, Terry Welker, said that the parlor has a policy of asking all customers how they want words spelled. He said if a customer agrees to a misspelling, "that falls back on them, not the artist."

Most spelling mistakes are not as financially costly as the one inflicted upon the unfortunate Mr. Williams, but they are often far more costly in other ways. Constantly combating misspellings on the job can take up time and energy that might otherwise be spent more productively, and misspelled words in personal and business correspondence can result in derision worse than that Mr. Williams endured. Misspellings can and do cost us money when, for example, we're passed up for a job because of errors on a cover letter or turned down for a loan because of a mistake-laden proposal. Bad spelling always reflects poorly on the writer, whether it's embedded in flesh or printed on a piece of paper. This is because we associate it with certain other (much more serious) negative attributes, like low intelligence, lack of education, and laziness.

But what does your spelling *really* say about you? Is spelling ability a measure of your education, intelligence, desire, or none of the above? A 1998 survey in *Parade* magazine's "Ask Marilyn" column focused on these very questions, and more than 42,000 people responded with their contributions to the data. The results indicated that our spelling has more to say about our organizational habits and other personality traits than our intelligence, which is great news for those of us whose spelling could use improvement—that is to say, all of us!

There is not one English speaker who can spell perfectly. What does this say about our language and about us, its creators? Have we created a monster, or is English spelling really less chaotic than it seems? There is both madness and method in our spelling system and in this book. The madness? A turbulent past, a complicated present, myriad effects on our emotions and thinking processes, and a flurry of technological attempts either to harness it all or hide from it. And the method? A personalized, logical approach to spelling improvement, designed to help you understand why spelling is such a challenge, recognize what patterns actually do exist in the words we use, and then meet the challenge head on. Such an approach will actively and systematically improve your spelling performance until you reach your goal, whether that goal is to graduate to the ranks of the excellent spellers, or to top the level of excellence you've already achieved.

PART ONE

The MADNESS

CHAPTER 1

SPELLING WELL:
The First Step to Graceful Communication

> Language is the archives of history.
> —RALPH WALDO EMERSON,
> essayist, poet, philosopher

> Language is a process of free creation; its laws and principles are fixed, but the manner in which the principles of generation are used is free and infinitely varied.
> —NOAM CHOMSKY,
> linguist, political analyst

If you're not a good speller, wouldn't you just love to have a literate argument for why you shouldn't even be *expected* to be a good speller? If so, read the next few chapters carefully, and you'll have more ammunition than you ever thought possible. And if you're an excellent speller, you can read them either in order to gloat silently, or in order to casually recite the facts at the next chic cocktail party to which you're invited, where you can use them to further infuriate everyone who is already jealous of your prowess. It'll be worth it.

What is the point of language, after all? The communication of higher thought. Without language, human beings would have no more culture than chimpanzees. (I know—we've all been to parties like that.) Talking would be limited to the basic exchanges necessary for survival and nothing more. Imagine asking the question: "Date tonight?" And getting the answer, "Ugh." But the mere presence of language capability doesn't guarantee the exchange of ideas—in order for communication to really happen, at least two people with language ability have to agree on a common language. Otherwise Billy-Bob's poetic description of the sunset, however intellectually evocative for Billy-Bob, will either have no effect whatsoever on Bobby-Joe, sounding like a series of meaningless grunts—or—worse, will approximate what in Bobby-Joe's language constitutes an insult and cause an abrupt end to the conversation. Or a few missing teeth. The key to communication is shared meaning. A system for encoding and decoding thoughts must be set as a standard and adhered to by both parties; otherwise, the meaning gets corrupted or lost en route.

But that standard isn't set in stone. On the contrary, language—like people—must change in order to survive and is, in fact, in a slow but constant state of flux. That's one of the apparently contradictory qualities of a language standard: it must be both an immutable authority and an ever-evolving reflection of cultural norms. Is this impossible? Not really. The seeming contradiction actually means merely that while rules change frequently, at any given point, there are still rules. Which is just the way we'd want it to work: standards that change with the times.

Another contradiction is that instead of just one universal standard, which would enable communication among all peoples, there are many. Did these numerous standards descend from a single original language? Or did they emerge independently? The question has been widely debated but is ultimately unanswerable because our written records go back only a fraction of the time during which human speech developed. Is this the way we would have planned it? Probably not. But who among us would really wish to drop all the world's languages in favor of one like Esperanto?

But even if we can't uncover the origin of language, we can at least investigate certain aspects of its recent development. Written records go as far back as a few thousand years B.C. and provide fascinating evidence for discovering how language standards evolve over time and how each and every one of us is part of that process. What becomes clear in studying this evidence is that new standards are born, not made, and that while we can exert great conscious and willful control over the documentation and dissemination of these standards, we can't, as individuals or as a society, consciously or substantively change them any more than we can change the weather. There are simply too many factors at work. We are truly adrift in a vast sea of words. No wonder it's so hard to spell them all.

Linguists identify the most dramatic cause of change in language as the isolation of "speech communities": groups of people who, as a result of forces like geographical distance, social and economic class, or getting clobbered by a rival, become disconnected from the larger society and form dialects of their own. In cases where the isolation is extreme—and maintained for long enough to be sufficiently documented in writing—an entirely new language emerges: a little like "twin talk" writ large. But if this were the only cause of change, language would now be at a standstill as modern communication technology has made this type of social isolation nearly impossible, and happily so. While the information revolution has had, to some degree, a homogenizing effect on language and will continue to do so, it is, in fact, the constant novelty of human experience that urges on the subtle transformation of language: each birth and death stirs the current. Shakespeare, in fact, was an extreme example of this, coining word after word after word.

The transmission of language to each new generation causes usage variations that become perceptible only after years and generations have passed, and then only if the latest version of the language is compared to one that is a century old or more. Generational change in language is not unlike what happens in a game of "telephone," in which each player passes on the message exactly as he or she hears it, but the message still changes dramatically during its travels from the first person to the last. Older people complain bitterly about the degradation of language, forgetting that they themselves took part in it!

The telephone game also demonstrates another point

about language change: that the spoken and written versions of a language are not just two different ways of expressing the same thing. Rather, they are two distinct entities. If that game of telephone is played using pen and paper instead of whispers and ears, the message arrives at the end virtually unchanged. Speech speeds up the fluctuation of language, and writing slows it down. But without either one, a language cannot survive.

The languages we now call "dead"—Latin, Ancient Greek, and Sanskrit—are actually merely dormant because they are no longer spoken. We may be able to speak them for scholarly purposes or for impressing our dates when we don't have much else going for us—using clues from the written forms of the languages—but conveyors of meaning that writing cannot record, such as pronunciation and intonation, are long gone. Most important, these languages are not spoken widely enough to foster change. If they were, they would rise from the dead to bedevil countless numbers of long-suffering schoolchildren who thought they had escaped from them permanently. And countless other languages that were spoken in the past but never written—or for which the written records have been lost—are dead to us now. A language must be both spoken *and* written in order to remain active and useful to the present culture.

The challenge, then, is to somehow reconcile these two necessary but opposing forces that make up a living language: writing, which promotes obscurity through stagnation, and speaking, which promotes obscurity through chaos. Think Laurel and Hardy. The place for this reconciliation is the dictionary, which—if written not just well, but magnificently—can bridge the gap between written and spoken standards. It can give new speech trends value by committing them to written form, and it can update written forms that have fallen out of use and keep them more in line with current speech. So, surprise! This function makes dictionaries the single most important factor in the creation of great literature. In the postscript of his book, *Dictionaries . . . : A Casebook on the Aims of Lexicographers and the Targets of Reviewers*, James Sledd remarks, "No man should let another choose his language for him; for speech and reason make us human. . . . We are not likely to choose well unless we know what we have to choose from. That is one reason why we need a descriptively accurate dictionary." The better the dictionary, the better our ability to communicate and create with language.

Fortunately or not, a dictionary is only as good as its creator, the lexicographer, and the idea that any one person or small group of people is in a position to steer the course of language standards is not just silly, it's troubling. It implies an inherent inequality—the assumption that only the usage preferred by the most powerful members of a society will be documented and preserved and that language itself is a tool for subjugating or eradicating the views and cultures of the less powerful members of society. Never fear. While this may have been true to a limited extent for the first dictionaries, in which the earliest lexicographers aimed to "fix" the language, it is less feasible a concern lately because the role of the lexicographer is now clearly defined as descriptive, not prescriptive: "A good dictionary is a guide to usage much as a good map tells you the nature of the terrain over which you may want to travel. It is not the function of the mapmaker to move rivers or rearrange mountains. . . ."—Clarence L. Barnhart, *American College Dictionary*

Jonathan Green adds, in *Chasing the Sun,* "the lexicographer is a historian, not a law-giver." Of course, plenty of historians—probably most—have been biased, and some have been just plain wrong. So we're nevertheless stuck with a controversy surrounding the idea of a standard, that its very existence creates a value system for language. In plain English: that which constitutes the standard is "good," and everything else is "bad." This scares some folks half to death. But it's not necessary to think of it in those stark terms. What determines a word's inclusion in the lexicon is its frequency of usage, not the socioeconomic status of its users, so inclusion is based on the democratic principle of majority rule. Americans can relax. Their beloved principles are not only not in danger, they are in charge. Moreover, there is ever–increasing documentation of new standards that deviate from the established norm but are nonetheless valid systems, and their documentation ultimately leads to increased usage that in turn leads to their inclusion in the "main" lexicon. Welcome to the modern world! Also, the idea that usages particular to specific sections of society are being purposefully, conspiratorially left out implies that language standards can be consciously designed, and history shows that this is false. No matter how much man has tried to change a language standard systematically and then keep it from growing—and mutating—on its own, he has never succeeded. And if he had, he'd be stuck with a dead language.

Dictionaries must be authoritative, not authoritarian, and this is no easy task. Note how tough it is to be a good parent to growing children. The challenge of writing a good dictionary is aptly described by Green: "In the end one is imprisoned in a vicious circle." The words in a language are the basis of the dictionary, but the dictionary has to be the basis of the words in a language. In this way, a standardized language depends on the existence of not just one good dictionary but many. The "perfect" dictionary would include every word ever used, its history, and its current meaning, but that dictionary does not exist. Instead, dictionaries have become more specialized in order to cover specific types of words or specific qualities of a more generalized group of words. Still, dictionaries like the *Oxford English Dictionary* (OED)—which is easily my personal favorite—approach the ideal.

While it would serve little purpose for a dictionary to include more than one word with *exactly* the same meaning, it serves great purpose to include many words that have *almost* the same meaning: words that denote the same concepts but signify subtle differences in connotation. This allows for subtlety of expression, a prerequisite for art. We have infinitely subtle thoughts, emotions, and experiences that we wish to convey, and a comparatively blunt instrument—language—with which to convey them. No matter how bright you may be, how many times have you tried to express your thoughts or your feelings to another, even the most receptive of friends or lovers, but failed utterly, nonetheless? So the more detailed and refined we can make our language, the better—provided, of course, that we keep it organized.

The key to this organization is a consistently upheld system of spelling. Spelling standards are essential to the flowering of a language because the effectiveness of a word and its various permutations of meaning depend on a specific spelling of that word. Otherwise, one person's "tow" would be another person's "toe." The labor of the lexicographer is in vain if these spellings are suddenly seen as interchangeable—not to mention the loss to our ability to communicate.

English spelling is unique in that it bears the marks of the near-countless standards that have converged to form it, making it the most culturally rich language in the world, the most diverse palette for literary exploration, and the biggest challenge to lexicographers. And spellers.

Many people believe that the "rules"—if you could call them that—of English spelling are unnecessarily complex and should be simplified. In fact, there have been simplified spelling movements for as long as there have been systems of spelling, but no one has yet been successful for the reason already mentioned: a living language is an independent organism, and its direction is beyond our ability to dictate. And there are strong arguments against the idea of spelling reform. Personally, I see simplification as akin to language-cleansing: getting rid of everything foreign and making the language much more "American" and easy to use. Well, good luck! Not only is this not a very pretty concept, it's probably impossible to achieve. If you're looking for something to do with the kids on a rainy Sunday afternoon, try creating your own system of spelling reform. This should give you enough to do until they've left for college. The end result will look like an entirely new language but much slimmer than before— like an abridged version of English.

And it won't be easy to read. For example, it's not always preferable for spellings to represent exactly the sound sequences in a word and nothing else. The words "cats," "dogs," and "horses" follow the same uniform spelling rule for forming the plural—adding an "s"—but in terms of pronunciation, the plural endings are all different. Phonetic spelling in this case would complicate things, not simplify them. In short, while such a system sounds good in theory, my best guess is that it would make things far more difficult in fact.

One of the strongest arguments against deliberate spelling reform designed to match spelling to pronunciation is that it would involve not just a single overhaul, but many. Because pronunciation and intonation (and their corresponding connotations and denotations) change slightly with each new generation, spelling rules would have to be redocumented and relearned several times in one person's lifetime. And you thought it was tough enough to learn all those rules? How would you like learning rules that *change*?

Dick Leith, in *A Social History of English*, presents a novel argument against a purely phonetic system: "A phonemic[1] spelling system can only hope to represent one accent, but the problem is whose? The selection of one discriminates, in principle, against speakers with other accents. By encoding the sounds of speech in an inconsistent and often arbitrary way, our spelling system at least manages to favour nobody. Contrary to what some people think, it is not a representation of the accent spoken by a small minority of the wealthy and priveleged.[2] We are all equally disadvantaged by it, and that is one of its strengths."

In practical terms, there is no ideal spelling standard. We can, and have, developed systems that seem much more logical than the one in present use, but the nature of language prevents these systems from being artificially introduced or imposed on current standards. In other words, even if we were somehow able to introduce a new system, it would eventually become just as chaotic as the present one because that is the natural course of events. Probably the best we can do for language (and by extension, culture) is to document the necessary complexities of meaning, grammar, and spelling as rigor-

1. A spelling system in which each letter corresponds directly to a particular phoneme. Phonemes are the individual sounds of a language. The number of phonemes in the English language is still under debate—perhaps because there are so many different ways of pronouncing it—but a common count is forty-four.
2. All material quoted throughout the book retains its original spelling. Therefore, British spellings (such as *favour* and *priveleged*, above) appear occasionally.

ously and as accurately as possible and ensure that at both the individual and societal level, the rules of organization are understood.

This process starts with your decision to read this book. In doing so, you are raising not only your own potential for using language but also the potential of the language itself.

CHAPTER 2

WHAT DOES YOUR SPELLING SAY ABOUT YOU? Some Compelling Reasons for Spelling Well

> My father still reads the dictionary every day. He says your life depends on your power to master words. —ARTHUR SCARGILL, British trades union leader

> For words, like Nature, half reveal
> And half conceal the Soul within.
> —ALFRED, LORD TENNYSON, British poet

Everything we do and say conveys a message about our personalities and ourselves. This is a terrifying realization. We're constantly sending signals out to the world—whether we're consciously aware of it or not—about our interests, backgrounds, states of mind, and just about everything else. But there's an enormous advantage to learning this: we can begin to control those signals. That is, we can change our actions and appearance to ensure that the message sent is the one intended, which is fairer both to us and to those with whom we interact. And seeing the positive results improves our self-esteem in the best possible way. We can finally see ourselves as worthwhile as we really are.

A good way to start improving, both professionally and personally, is to notice how we're representing ourselves on paper because writing is just as important a mode of communication as face-to-face interaction or conversations on the phone but easier to control. The latter two happen in "real time," but a written correspondence can be thought out, developed, and polished before the recipient ever sees it—even with an instant message, you choose when to send your words—which makes it a great opportunity for presenting oneself in the best possible light. (Consider your experiences online.) And passing up this opportunity means giving up control over what happens at the other end, opening up the possibility that the writing won't do justice to the writer.

There are plenty of ways to improve your writing, but the most basic and straightforward (and consequently the most often overlooked) is perfecting your spelling. You can't carry your electronic spell-checker around in your head, and a single clunker, depending on what it is, can blow your image. (Some spelling errors look dreadful; others are common even to good spellers.) When your spelling is perfect, it is invisible—the reader has no reason to notice it unless it's wrong. But when it goes wrong, it spurs strong associations in the mind of the reader, even when he or she isn't aware of them. These associations run from major (like a lack of general intelligence) to minor (such as a lack of attention to detail), but they nearly always cause the reader to form a negative view about the writer's inherent abilities, and they certainly cast an unflattering light on the written piece as a whole. As David Moseley observes in his survey of current spelling research in Gordon Brown and Nick Ellis's *Handbook of Spelling*, "From Theory to Practice: Errors and Trials," "Inaccurate spelling triggers a heightened sensitivity to other weaknesses in composition." He goes on to say that this phenomenon may cause many bright people to be prevented from realizing their full potential because the resulting criticism reflects on the writing (or worse, on the person) as a whole, instead of the spelling in particular.

Recently, a letter to my "Ask Marilyn" column in *Parade*, the Sunday magazine, questioned whether spelling ability is a measure of education, intelligence, desire, or none of the above. To help answer the question, I conducted a reader survey, which drew well over 42,000 responses. The results supported my theory that spelling performance has less correlation with intelligence than we might fear, but it does have some correlation with certain (happily, modifiable) personality traits. Here's the original survey that appeared in the magazine and its results.

THE ASK MARILYN SURVEY

Dear Marilyn:

Do you believe that the ability to spell is a measure of education, intelligence, or desire? I have a Ph.D. from Texas A&M University, but I needed my computer spell-checker to correctly spell two words in this letter, and I suspect that many of your intelligent and educated readers are spelling-impaired, also. I wish I could spell. If no one has done a study on this, perhaps you could help.

—Michael K. Mitchell, Anchorage, Alaska

I have a theory about bad spelling, but it's based only on personal observation. To see if it's valid, I need information from more people. Readers, would you like to take part? Whether your spelling is almost perfect, or it could use a lot of improvement, get out a pencil and answer the following questions. Be as honest as you can bear. You can remain anonymous.

Bad spellers of the world, unite! Are you tired of feeling foolish, avoiding writing anything down, and hiding behind your computer program's automatic spell-checker? Are you secretly appalled when you see that you can't even get through a few paragraphs without yet another embarrassing reminder popping up on the screen? Let's go to work on finding out why. Participate in the following "Spelling Survey" by writing the numbers 1 through 15 on a piece of paper, then answering the following questions.

The Spelling Survey

Rate yourself *compared to others* on a scale from 1 to 100, with 100 as the highest rating:

1. Where would you rank yourself as a speller?

2. Where would you rank your leadership ability?

3. Where would you rank your ability to follow instructions?

4. Where would you rank as a creative person?

5. Where would you rank as an organized person?

6. Where would you rank your ability to solve problems?

Choose the answer that more closely applies to you:

7. When you have trouble balancing your checkbook, do you . . .
   A) Keep at it until you account for every penny? (or)
   B) Give up and correct your balance to match the bank's?

8. Which better describes your housekeeping habits?
   A) "A place for everything, and everything in its place."
   B) "At my place, everything is all over the place."

9. In most matters of the mind, are you . . .
   A) As patient as you can be? (or)
   B) As decisive as you can be?

10. With regard to time management, do you . . .
    A) Prioritize as best you can? (or)
    B) Have no time to think about it?

11. When you're not in a rush to get to work, do you . . .
    A) Make up your bed every day? (or)
    B) Consider the whole concept silly?

Again, rate yourself *compared to others* on a scale from 1 to 100, with 100 as the highest rating:

12. Where would you rank your spelling of words?

13. Where would you rank your spelling of names?

14. Where would you rank your pronunciation of words?

15. Where would you rank your pronunciation of names?

The Survey Reporting

Note: Our experiment was not a scientific poll. First, only readers who wished to participate did so, so the data were reported selectively. Second, the participants' assessments of themselves were subjective, so one good speller might be different from another good one. Here's how I handled these concerns. First, because readers reported selectively, numbers were not reported. That is, it was not reported that "n *percent* of Americans are good spellers." Second, because readers assessed themselves, labels were not reported. That is, it was not reported that "n percent of Americans are *good* spellers." Instead, relationships were noted.

THE SURVEY RESULTS

Dear Marilyn:
A reader asked if you believe that spelling ability is a measure of education, intelligence, or desire. I was fascinated by the survey you published in response. The implication of the questions is that you believe spelling ability may be related to personality. What were the results? I'm dying to know.
—Judith Alexander, Chicago, Illinois

The biggest (and best) news is this: the result of our spelling experiment—in which 42,603 readers took part (20,188 by postal mail and 22,415 by e-mail)—indicates that poor spelling ability apparently has no relationship to general intelligence.

On the other hand, education, intelligence, and desire *must* have a relationship to *excellent* spelling ability: if one has little education, intelligence, and desire, one will surely not be able to spell. But my theory is that even if one has the basics, one's personality traits may still stand in the way. Or perhaps one's traits may boost one into the ranks of excellent spellers—in particular, the trait for being meticulous.

Readers were first asked to rank their spelling ability on a scale of 1 to 100. Choosing an answer established a personal assessment range for each individual. Readers were then asked to rank other traits on that same range. In my analysis, I first noted an individual's spelling rank and then noted which other quality he or she ranked closest to his or her spelling rank.

I considered that quality—or qualities—to be the most closely related to the individual's spelling ability. This greatly reduced the effect of subjectivity in self-assessment. In other words, I may not know what an individual means by ranking his spelling ability as, say, 75, but *he* does. So no matter what his actual ability is, and no matter how accurately he managed to assess it, I could still determine the quality that related to it more closely than anything else, for that individual. By ranking other qualities on the same scale, he pointed it out himself. I call this technique "self-normalization."

The answer to "Where would you rank your ability to follow instructions?" (which is a personality trait interacting with general intelligence) related most often to spelling ability. It was followed by "Where would you rank your ability to solve problems?" (which is general intelligence alone). And this was followed by "Where would you rank as an organized person?" (which is a personality trait alone).

Here's the good news: The first two relationships were top-heavy, meaning that they related strongly for top spellers, but hardly at all for bottom spellers. In fact, of the worst spellers, only 6 percent ranked their ability to follow instructions closest to their spelling ability, and only 5 percent ranked their ability to solve problems closest to it.

But one of the three significant relationships was consistent from the top spellers down to the bottom spellers: organizational ability. The top spellers were the most organized, the average spellers were in the middle, and the bottom spellers were the least organized. In other words, organization paralleled spelling ability closest of all.

In short, here's what this means: Our experiment indicates that if you're a top speller, you're more likely to be more intelligent than average, better able to follow instructions than average, and more organized than average. On the other hand, if you're a bottom speller, your general intelligence and ability to follow instructions are *not likely* to be lower than average, but you are *more likely* to be less organized. This result suggests it is possible that a lack of organization drags a speller down.

I included the question "Where would you rank your leadership ability?" only to validate my methods because I was confident that leadership ability has nothing to do with spelling ability. This was borne out by the data: it related least often. I also included the question "Where would you rank as a creative person?" because I doubted that creativity had anything to do with spelling ability (or the lack of it), but I still was curious about it: it related virtually the same.

The following results are not categorized by spelling ability, and are just for fun:

• When they have trouble balancing their checkbooks, 59 percent of the readers who responded give up and change their balance to match the bank's.

• About housekeeping habits, 65 percent of those responding say, "At my place, everything is all over the place."

• In most matters of the mind, 89 percent call themselves decisive.

• With regard to time management, 52 percent have no time to think about it.

• And even when they're not in a hurry to get to work, 81 percent of our respondents don't make their beds every day.

We sure sound like rushed, resolute Americans, don't we?! In the best spellers, however, noticeable differences are found everywhere except in the area of decisiveness:

• When they have trouble balancing their checkbooks, only 36 percent of them (instead of 59 percent) give up. The other 64 percent keep at it until they account for every penny.

• About housekeeping habits, only 49 percent (instead of 65 percent) admit to being a bit messy. The other 51 percent maintain, "A place for everything, and everything in its place."

• With regard to time management, only 34 percent (instead of 52 percent) have no time to think about it. The other 66 percent prioritize as best they can.

• And when they're not in a hurry to get to work, only

57 percent (instead of 81 percent) don't make their beds. The rest do.

(On a side note, no useful observations were generated from the answers to questions 12 through 15, which were about the spelling and pronunciation of words and names.)

In sum, it appears that spelling ability may be more related to personality traits or habits than has been assumed. What to do about it? Keep in mind that the difference between a good speller and a bad speller is not huge: just a few letters here and there. Yes, I'm serious. Remember that even bad spellers can spell most words perfectly. I suggest being more meticulous about spelling: that is, try harder. If you work on a computer, go ahead and use your spell-checker, but whenever it finds a misspelled word, stop and hand-write the correct spelling a dozen times. If you don't work on a computer, keep a dictionary handy. Whenever you're not sure of how to spell a word, don't guess! Look it up first. Then write it down a dozen times. If you do this without fail for the next six months, your spelling will improve dramatically.

So it's great news about spelling and intelligence. But most significant of all is that so many readers took part in a spelling experiment. What does this say about us? It says that we're tremendously interested in matters of the mind. It says that we're interested in way more than movie stars and fashion. And as for myself, I think it says that Americans are being under-estimated. Thanks a million for your help.

The conclusions suggested by the results of this survey are both fascinating and encouraging because they challenge some of the stereotypes we have about bad spellers. First, they show the relationship between spelling and intelligence to be anything but predictable. That's good news for those of us who feared that our bad spelling was an indicator of low intelligence. Second, they suggest that the relationship between spelling ability and organizational habits is, for this survey at least, surprisingly linear: as stated in the column, "The top spellers were the most organized, the average spellers were in the middle, and the bottom spellers were the least organized." This suggests that the difference between a poor speller and a good speller may be, in many cases, a few counterproductive (but perhaps reversible) habits.

These conclusions—specifically regarding spelling and intelligence—can be easily misunderstood, so a fuller explanation follows. Instead of suggesting that spelling ability has no correlation with intelligence at all, the survey suggests a different, more subtle relationship between the two:

1. *We can safely say that excellent spelling ability nearly always indicates high intelligence; however, high intelligence doesn't necessarily produce excellent spelling ability.*
2. *Likewise, we can safely say that low intelligence nearly always produces poor spelling ability; however, poor spelling ability doesn't necessarily indicate low intelligence.*

The first statement indicates that while excellent spelling ability can't exist (except in rare cases) without high intelligence, high intelligence exists without excellent spelling ability. This suggests that something other than intelligence can affect spelling ability. The second statement shows that while low intelligence is almost always accompanied by poor spelling, poor spelling is found in people of all intelligence levels. Again, we're left with the conclusion that some other factors must be at work in determining spelling ability.

The notion that poor spelling doesn't indicate low intelligence but may instead indicate the presence of bad habits is encouraging for those of us who wish to improve our spelling, and happily, it is supported not just by the results of this survey but by evidence from psycholinguistic research as well.

A good deal of research has been devoted to investigating the connections—or lack of them—between spelling ability and general intelligence, and the verdict is clear: one cannot reliably predict the other. For starters, the phrase "spelling ability" is almost a misnomer as spelling is probably not an inherent aptitude but, rather, an acquired skill, as the Johnson O'Connor Research Foundation suggested in its 1992 report entitled "The Spelling Project." Here is a summary of its results: "The strongest relationships for spelling ability were with English vocabulary, reading efficiency, number checking, age, and years of education. . . . Although there may be distinct aptitudes or other dispositions that affect spelling ability, spelling itself appears to be a learned skill and not an inherent aptitude." This assertion is encouraging for people who consider themselves to be "born losers" where spelling is concerned. After all, how could there possibly be a "spelling gene"? There's no such thing as spelling in the world of nature.

Beyond that, evidence provided by numerous studies indicates that the relationship between general intelligence and spelling ability is unpredictable. Here's what some of the experts say. David Moseley states, "Spelling is not a reliable index of general intelligence, as dyslexics with specific spelling problems often remind us. Crawford (1992) found that spelling scores and verbal intelligence had only 21% of variance in common and still lower correlation coefficients have been reported in the literature for younger children." Margaret Snowling, in her contribution to the *Handbook of Spelling* entitled "Towards a Model of Spelling Acquisition: The Development of Some Component Skills," makes these remarks about spelling and intelligence: "Our experience leads us to suggest that deficits in phonological (sound-to-spelling) processing . . . have a more devastating effect upon spelling development than other sorts of cognitive difficulty, including low intelligence." Linda Siegel, in her contribution to the *Handbook of Spelling* entitled "The Modularity of Reading and Spelling: Evidence from Hyperlexia," states, "A small percentage of reported cases of hyperlexia (a rare condition in which a child has advanced reading skills in spite of severe language and cognitive deficits) have been found to have extraordinary spelling skills. The presence of these superior skills creates problems for assumptions about the importance of cognitive and linguistic factors in spelling."

So, if bad spelling doesn't indicate low intelligence, what *does* it indicate? For many people, it indicates a deficiency in pronunciation skills. Nata Goulandris says, in her contribution to *The Handbook of Spelling* entitled "Teaching Spelling: Bridging Theory and Practice," "Phonological skills are vital when learning to spell because they enable children to understand the alphabetic link between the sounds heard in spoken words and the letters used to represent them in written language." Interestingly, researchers have suggested that musical training, with specific focus on rhythm and pitch, can help improve spelling skills by stimulating phonological activity. But growing up with less-than-perfect phonology skills doesn't preclude your ability to be a good speller. What it may mean is that some psychological adaptation must take place to make up for the deficiency. Luckily, human beings are extremely adaptable creatures. (Otherwise, how could people like me, who grew up in the rolling hills of the Midwest, learn to love living in a high-rise in New York City, where the closest thing to a lake is the West Side highway after a really big rain?)

Some research suggests that good and poor spellers actually use different psychological processes to spell the same words. Carolyn Lennox and others in a contribution to *Reading and Spelling: Development and Disorders*, entitled "Phonological and orthographic processes in good and poor spellers" assert, "Good spellers use both phonological and visual cues to a greater extent than do age-matched poor spellers. However, when poor spellers approach difficult words, they will more likely rely on their well-developed visual memory skills, whereas good spellers will rely on their well-developed phonological skills."

It is believed that poor spellers, who don't have a good capacity for assembling the spelling of a word from its basic phonetic components, must rely more heavily on a stored memory of what that particular word looks like. This is why good spellers are much more adept than poor spellers at spelling words they've only heard spoken but never (or rarely) seen written down. Moseley says, ". . . a good speller can spell a great many words, irrespective of spelling regularity and even if a word's meaning is not fully understood. Good spellers can spell new words by analogy, applying a wide range of linguistic principles, some of which they may have acquired through using dictionaries. They also make use of word-specific knowledge, which they acquire not only through the application of intelligence but in habitual and repetitive ways."

So maybe lessons for spelling improvement can be taken from noting behavior common among good spellers. In a study entitled "Lessons from Champion Spellers," J. W. Logan and others discovered some frequent traits of excellent spellers: Champion spellers were highly motivated and self-disciplined, and they showed strong control over their own learning. Most used three main spelling strategies: visual memory, writing or saying words aloud, and regular use of the dictionary. In other words, merely trying harder may help. Another study found that good handwriting was a key factor in promoting the visual perception of word form, reporting that good spellers wrote swiftly and legibly.

But relax. Jody-Anne Maxwell, the winner of the 1998 Scripps Howard National Spelling Bee, received an impressive array of prizes for her efforts, but as Lise Hoffman recounted in her article for *The Saturday Evening Post*, all those rewards couldn't distract Jody-Anne from the more important things in life: "All the loot aside, what was Jody-Anne's favorite part of the Scripps Howard Spelling Bee? 'The sitting down,' she says. 'At the national finals in Jamaica, we had to stand for seven hours.'"

As early as 1901, studies investigating the causes of bad spelling indicated that good spelling was not a mysterious aptitude mysteriously acquired, but a specific set of learned skills, instead. A study cited by David Russell in his book *Characteristics of Good and Poor Spellers* makes a distinction between general and specific abilities: "In 1901, in a study of the causes of chronic bad spelling, Carmen concluded that 'Ability to spell well . . . probably implies not a general habit or power of observation, but a special ability to notice small differences in words.'" These results are encouraging because they suggest that spelling excellence, far from being any kind of genetically pre-ordained quality, is simply a skill that, like all other skills, requires motivation, discipline, and practice to master. Which makes spelling well no different from doing anything else well: *attainable*.

One interesting finding is that low self-esteem often accompanies bad spelling. David Moseley describes a study reporting that "poor spelling is associated with a poor concept of the self as a writer and . . . peer counseling on self-image, locus of control, and spelling led to improved spelling, reading, and handwriting as well as producing some attitudinal and social gains."

And low self-esteem can manifest itself in a wide range of counterproductive behavior, including procrastination, lack of ability to focus on the task at hand, apathy, and lack of organization, all of which can sabotage spelling ability and can persist as bad habits even after self-image is improved. So maybe it's no wonder that the two are related. According to the results of a study entitled "Can Discrepancies Between IQ and Basic Skills Be Explained By Learning Strategies?," other counterproductive behavior associated with spelling difficulty includes a tendency to work too quickly and an aversion to reflection or feedback.

A study conducted in 1994 by Joan Rankin and others, entitled "The Development of Beliefs About Spelling and Their Relationship to Spelling Performance," found an interesting relationship between the participants' beliefs about spelling in general and their own spelling ability specifically and the participants' actual performance on tests: "Students with high efficacy as spellers and high outcome expectancy of spelling for writing were the best spellers, with the highest performance reserved for those who attributed good spelling more to effort than ability." Another study published the same year, entitled "Spelling Skills and Causal Attributions in Children," indicated that adolescents with below-average spelling skills were more likely to attribute a low score on a spelling test to a lack of ability, which, according to the authors of the study, "predisposed them to a helpless orientation that prevented them from overcoming their difficulties," whereas the above-average spellers were more likely to attribute the failure to "luck,"[1] indicating a higher degree of confidence in ability. Interesting! Is it possible that when you think you can better yourself, you can? And when you think you can't, you can't?

The idea that expectations and opinions of yourself can measurably affect your performance is not so surprising, but concrete evidence for it with regard to spelling is revolutionary: it opens up a whole new avenue of spelling improvement for people who have always considered themselves "hopeless at spelling." We now can feel confident that the mere act of becoming hopeful can help to turn that pattern around.

Uta Frith, in her foreword to the *Handbook of Spelling*, characterizes the psychological challenges of spelling this way: "According to some estimates a reasonably literate person has at least 50,000 words at their fingertips. How are these words represented in the mind? How are we able to call on them at a instant's notice? How do we learn their orthographic patterns and remember them for a lifetime? . . . The puzzle of spelling is only made more puzzling when we think about breakdowns in this process."

---

1. The full study was not available at this writing. Judging from the information provided in the abstract, a "luck" attribution may mean that the students blamed the low scores on the fact that the particular words selected for the test were unfamiliar and felt confident that given a different set of words, they would have received higher scores.

Q & A WITH UTA FRITH

Uta Frith is a Professor in Cognitive Development at University College London. She is the editor of the pioneering book *Cognitive Processes in Spelling* (1980) and the author of two books on autism.

MvS: *There's an ever-expanding body of evidence support-ing the idea that intelligence is not of major importance to spelling ability in the average adult. Other factors, ranging from phonological skills to self-esteem to atten-tion to detail, have been proposed as having greater influ-ence. What does your experience lead you to conclude about the primary determinants of spelling ability?*

UF: "Self-esteem" is often bandied about, but I doubt that it can explain anything. Perhaps it is an indi-rect step in a learning process: maybe you decide to put a high value on spelling skill. (Cultural factors are important here—what your social environment has conditioned you to think and expect.) In this case, not being able to spell would diminish your self-esteem. . . . This may then give you a strong motivation to learn strategies to overcome your dif-ficulty. Attention to detail is an interesting informa-tion-processing style, about which we know little. It is possible that if we had good measures for "atten-tion to detail," these would correlate with spelling skill. However, this would not apply to individuals with dyslexia.

MvS: *Do you believe that anyone of average (or greater) intelligence can improve his or her spelling, regardless of his or her current level of ability?*

UF: Yes, average or greater intelligence can be used to devise strategies that overcome problems. If the motivation is there, then this would result in improvement. However, the improvement is something like a "trick"—it is not the same as the performance of naturally good spellers, who don't need tricks. They remember words willy-nilly. In contrast, the strategic improvements that are possible for poor spellers come at a considerable cost. The costs may be too great in some cases. Also, the skill falls to pieces if there are other demands on information-processing at the same time.

MvS: *How, in your opinion, can an awareness of the psychological processes at work in spelling help us to improve our spelling?*

UF: Awareness of language processes probably works for good spellers and possibly for super-intelligent poor spellers. I believe that you are likely to be a good speller if you have a deep interest in language, its roots, the connections between different words via meaning and via sound, and generally the poetic quality of words. However, which is the chicken and which is the egg? You can't conjure up the interest unless you already have some basic talent. I am a great believer in spell-checkers and other aids, which I recommend to children and adults with difficulties. This, in my opinion, is a far preferable and more intelligent use of resources than extra training and tuition. However, a few lessons often work wonders—just to explain the basics of English orthography. English-speaking people need to be made aware of the complexity of the orthographic system of their language. Speakers of languages such as Italian or Spanish have a far easier time learning to spell.

Chris M. Sterling, in the introduction to *Psychology, Spelling and Education*, says of spelling, "Explaining why people have problems with it is easier than explaining how they became proficient in its use. . . ." So why does spelling, and English spelling in particular, present such a psychological challenge? Because although English orthography is an alphabetic system, it is not an ideal one—and far from it! If it were ideal (phonetically speaking), there would be one letter to represent each sound; instead, there are forty-four elementary sounds (called phonemes) in the English language, with only twenty-six letters to represent them, so each letter (and, more confusingly, different combinations of letters) can represent any of several different sounds depending on the context. And the evolution of the English language has complicated the rules of this representation, merging words and word forms from other languages so that the current orthography is a mixture of standards: some spellings are phonetically based, others are dictated by nonphonetic rules, and still others are aberrations that have nevertheless become accepted by virtue of their inclusion in dictionaries over the years. In plain English: yikes! (Yikes is a word of dubious origin and even more dubious value in usage, but would you get rid of it? I wouldn't. And at least it's easy to spell!)

There are, nevertheless, arguments in favor of the current orthography, which maintain that despite its illogical appearance—and that's putting it mildly—the English spelling system is actually quite well-suited to its purpose. Chief among them is the following, from *The Sound Pattern of English* by Noam Chomsky and Morris Halle: "Orthography is a system designed for readers who know the language, who understand sentences and therefore know the surface structure of sentences. Such readers can

produce the correct phonetic forms, given the orthographic representation and the surface structure, by
means of the rules that they employ in producing and
interpreting speech. . . . It is therefore noteworthy, but
not too surprising, that English orthography, despite its
often cited inconsistencies, comes remarkably close to
being an optimal orthographic system for English." Okay,
I didn't call it a *strong* argument, did I?

Margaret Peters, in her contribution to *Psychology,
Spelling and Education* entitled "Towards Spelling Auton-
omy," presents an interesting defense for the English
spelling system, asserting that in terms of probability of
letter sequences, it is "by no means irregular." Really?!
Her argument is as follows: "The orthography consists of
a vast number of letter sequences, many of which have
varied pronunciations. As in the grammar of a language
where there is a stronger possibility of some words occur-
ring next in a sequence than there is of others, so it is
with strings of letters. It is an example of what is known
as the stochastic process, which is any process governed
by the laws of probability. In the case of the language
process the expected probability of occurrence of any single element in sequence, from the point of view of the
reader or listener, is governed by the immediate context
and his or her previous personal experience of similar
kinds of context. Now far from being the unsystematic,
unpredictable collection of words handed down from a
muddled and motley collection of etymological sources,
spelling is just another example of this stochastic
process." If this is true, we've just explained why most
disorganized closets look the way they do.

The arguments of Chomsky/Halle and Peters place
emphasis on the view of orthography as primarily a
visual, written system, designed for skilled users of the
language who have internalized the common phonetic

aspects of the language. From this linguistic perspective, it seems to make sense. But the question that remains is exactly how we skilled users of the language accomplish such complex tasks.

The coexistence in English orthography of phonetic, nonphonetic, and aberrational spellings, and the requisite thought processes it suggests, led to the development by psycholinguists of the "dual-process model"—a theoretical representation of two psychological pathways for accessing spelling information—to explain how the brain is able to master and retain such a complicated system. In the dual-process model, the first of the two pathways—the phonological route—breaks up a word into the individual phonemes that comprise it, then uses knowledge of sound-to-spelling or phoneme-to-grapheme correspondences to come up with the appropriate spelling. The second pathway—the lexical route—deals with words that defy phonetic rules by accessing a word store, or lexicon, and retrieving the specific information needed for an idiosyncratic spelling. Evidence that these two routes exist and can function independently of each other has been found through the study of brain damage and its effects on spelling ability. Specifically, scientists in the field of cognitive neuropsychology have been able to determine from the types of spelling errors made by brain-damaged people that in some cases the damage has only affected one route and not the other.

Recently, however, the idea that these two routes are independent in normal brain function has been convincingly challenged. Christopher Barry, in his contribution to *Psychology, Spelling and Education* entitled "Interactions Between Lexical and Assembled Spelling (In English, Italian and Welsh)," presents the argument clearly: The neuropsychological dissociations found in the inability to write show clearly that the routes are *sep-*

arable: neurological damage can selectively impair one functional spelling system and leave the other relatively intact. However, whether the two routes are functionally independent in normal spellers—who are assumed to possess both—is a different question.

Answers to this question and others are now being approached through the use of computational models[2] to track the paths of all the possible thought processes English spelling can inspire. Evidence from these computational models has spawned what are known as "connectionist" theories, which challenge and expand the traditional dual-route model by demonstrating other possibilities, among them that one route might be capable of accomplishing both phonological (sound-based) and lexical (deriving from stored knowledge of specific words) spelling tasks. (More discussion of these computational models can be found in Chapter Five.)

Gaining a little understanding of the psychological machinery at work in the task of spelling helps us not only to visualize these mental processes but also to appreciate what an astonishing achievement it is to have mastered English orthography, the most difficult spelling system in the world. In short: don't feel so bad when you misspell a word. Even those who consider themselves "bad" spellers need to understand that they've already accomplished quite a lot and that the step up from their current level of spelling performance to the ranks of excellent spelling is a relatively small one. Best of all, it's clear that the momentum required for making that step is already at our command. We need only to realize it's there to begin making use of it.

2. Computational models for spelling are theoretical respresentations of the cognitive processes involved in spelling tasks, expressed mathematically using computers.

CHAPTER **3**

THE SPELLING BRAIN

As long as our brain is a mystery, the universe, the reflection of the structure of the brain, will also be a mystery. —SANTIAGO RAMON Y CAJAL, Spanish scientist

The brain has muscles for thinking, as the legs have muscles for walking.
—JULIEN OFFROY DE LA METTRIE, French philosopher

When one thinks of champion spellers, the image that comes to mind is a spelling bee, with participants lined up on a stage and spelling out all those mind-boggling words that are read to them by an announcer. But this activity involves a completely different set of pathways in the brain than the type of spelling most of us do every day in our business correspondence and personal letters. To spell words that are spoken to us, we must first make sense of the spoken sounds. Depending on how the brain in question has stored the word (or not stored it, if the word is unfamiliar), one of several things can happen: (1) the sounds may be matched up with the correct orthographic segments to build the word (if it is unfamiliar), which would employ the smaller set of structures in the left hemisphere that governs word-formation; or (2) they may be compared with the lexicon of known words stored within that same word-form network so that the matching word can then be retrieved and spelled; or (3) the spoken word may trigger a non-language memory—a connection formed between the word and an abstract concept or physical sensation—in which case the spelling must be accessed via the larger network of neurons responsible for storing nonlanguage interactions between the body and its environment. What a feat! Yet we all do it every day.

A SPELLING BEE FOR ADULTS

The differences between the feats performed in spelling bees and "everyday" spelling activity aren't limited to pathways in the brain: There's also a big difference between the types of words that pop up at work or at home and those that buzz around spelling bees. Edith Pearlman's article for *Smithsonian* entitled "We May Be Temerarious and Unsuasible, But Can We Orthographize?" portrays one particular spelling bee for adults. As she describes it, "A gleeful audience pays cash to watch the hapless contestants shoehorn an extra *e* into 'eleemosynary' and mix up the consonants in 'fuchsia.'. . ."

Here's her summary of the evening's festivities: "The academics couldn't agree about 'suffrutescent' and went down wrangling. The patriarchs sailed through 'gurney.' Three teams had now been eliminated. In the second round, the doctors got 'bradawl' and the patriarchs 'degauss.' On the third round, the doctors missed 'crocheting,' and the patriarchs triumphed with 'wirrah,' everybody's favorite fish. Our match was over. All 15 of us, foes no longer, descended from the stage chattering and, in some cases, scratching. 'This damned gown has some kind of ectoparasite,' fussed one of the academics. 'Siphonaptera,' clarified [another]. 'Fleas,' said Sasha, smiling at last."

Written spelling, on the other hand, involves the translation of abstract concepts into word forms and the stimulation of those structures in the brain that allow the hand to direct the pen on the page (or the keys on the keyboard). But this is only true for spontaneous writing, as in writing a letter or a story. Different routes are accessed when we're copying from another written source. In this case, we either read the words to be copied, translate them into concepts, and then translate them back into orthographic forms, or we copy the visual forms of letters directly without accessing their abstract concept equivalents at all. Did you ever have the feeling, like when you're trying to study something boring, that you've looked at the words, but you haven't actually read them? It's something like that.

The view of the "spelling brain" that is emerging is an encouraging one because it portrays the spelling system as a kind of maze, which, for the good speller, has well-worn paths that are easy to follow and, for the poor speller, has obstacles blocking certain paths. But in both cases, the system contains the same amount of information—it's just a question of clearing the pathways or creating new ones. Researchers in the area of spelling recovery have used this newfound understanding of the specific routes for spelling and the circumstances that trigger them in order to help people with spelling disorders learn to circumvent their obstructed paths by using a process of association.

You probably don't have a "spelling disorder," but take note, anyway: individuals are instructed to link a word that they spell easily with one that they don't, thereby "borrowing" the route of the familiar word to access the spelling for the unfamiliar word. Another method found to be useful is associating problem words with visual images or abstract concepts that are easily recalled, thereby circumventing the formal, lexical route and accessing the spelling via the conceptual route, instead. Fascinating stuff. My guess is that most—maybe all—of us are using mental processes like these, both routinely and unconsciously, but with much more than spelling: rather, we're doing this with all sorts of tasks that relate to learning and performance. In other words, we each have our own methods of getting through the day's thinking.

Other findings helpful for spelling instruction and improvement include the results of a 1995 study comparing the spelling performance and learning ability of average spellers in the morning to the afternoon and finding the morning to be a better time for both performance and learning, especially for those types of words that access systems in the left hemisphere. Knowing that the left hemisphere is better engaged in the morning indicates that performance and learning related to other language skills may be better early in the day as well. So habits developed and ingrained may have made a difference, too.

So you say you can't spell? Don't worry: it's all in your head. The human brain, headquarters for not only the functions of the body but also the less tangible yet no less real functions of the mind, has been an endless source of fascination for us since we first became aware of its existence. This fascination has only increased with each new piece of information we have gleaned about its function. But obtaining that information is no easy task. After all, how can we peer inside the head of a living human being? We can get some of our questions answered by studying the brains of animals, but in the case of language, the only brains that will provide real answers are our own. And those are turning out to be immensely more complicated than we'd ever thought. It often seems that the more we learn, the less we know.

The challenge, then, is to find a way to study the brain without interfering with its function. The first such method to be discovered—analyzing changes in behavior and ability following damage to the brain—is evident in Pharaonic medical texts from around 3000 B.C. (not long after the birth of written language in the West) and is still commonly used today. In fact, despite the considerable technological achievements of the last fifty years, such analysis remains one of the most informative methods available for studying the function of the brain, especially considering the sheer volume of data it has yielded over so many thousands of years. And this goes to show us how vast must be the amount of information that we're lacking.

Those observations that relate specifically to language derive from the documentation of a disorder known as aphasia. Aphasia is a blanket term, used to describe any deficit of language following brain injury. So the category contains a wide range of symptoms and injuries, from mild to severe. The value of studying cases of aphasia is that the damage isolates areas of the brain and links them to certain abilities, by virtue of their being impaired. And by keeping track of where the system breaks down and what effects this breakdown has on the system's function, we can come to establish causal links between the two and form a map of sorts, indicating which functions are governed where. As Alfonso Caramazza puts it in a 1995 interview with the *Journal of Cognitive Neuroscience*, "Brain damage unpacks the closely integrated normal system to reveal its internal structure." An analogy for this process would be turning off one light switch after another on a panel of many switches and taking note of which lights go off as a result. In theory, this method of discovering connections is fine; in fact, it's not so simple. The relationship between the structure of our brains and our abilities and behavior is not so direct, nor is it predictable from one person to another. Each of us has his or her own panel of switches that is constantly being rewired. The most complicated computer imaginable is like an abacus by comparison.

The brain is an amazingly adaptive—and maladaptive—network of nerves that is constantly modifying its connections, both internally and in relation to the rest of the nervous system, according to the particular experiences and needs of the mind and body they govern. So in this respect, brains are as individual as fingerprints. Yet they are not without similarities. Just as there are certain qualities we have come to expect in all human noses (e.g., there tends to be only one per person, and I think we can all be thankful for this—consider the last time you had a bad cold) and certain other qualities that we understand are greatly variable (e.g., size and shape), many aspects of the brain are predictable, and many are certainly not.

It makes sense, then, that while some patterns appear among the statistics concerning the location of language in the brain, these patterns are neither uniform nor universal. For instance, current evidence indicates that for 99 percent of right-handed people, language functions are controlled predominantly by the left hemisphere of the brain. But only about 60 percent of left-handed and ambidextrous people have language "centers" in the left hemisphere. About 30 percent have language-dominant right hemispheres, and the remaining 10 percent have language represented in both hemispheres. The idea that the brain might be mapped out like a schematic for the engine of a car, with every portion sectioned off and named for the tasks it performs, is not such a bad one—

indeed, we have managed to make at least some designations about where the brain activity responsible for certain functions can usually be found—but it's easy to let ourselves get drawn into simplistic thinking, even when such thinking appears complex. The understandable desire to categorize our behavior into types and then assign these types to specific and isolated regions of the brain leads us to incorrect assumptions, some of them notorious. Such was the pitfall of the phrenologists, a group of physicians in the early nineteenth century who, in their zeal to understand and explain the processes of the brain, ended up espousing some hilariously unscientific ideas, but who nevertheless provided an impetus for the more serious pursuit of a localization of language processes in the brain.

Phrenology centered around the idea that particular talents and personality traits were governed by clearly delineated areas of the brain and that those areas would be either more or less developed, depending on an individual's innate gifts and propensities, and that the well-developed areas caused actual bumps in the skull. So it was believed that close examination of a person's skull could reveal truths about his or her nature. A chief contributor to the movement was a Viennese doctor named Franz-Joseph Gall, whose original diagram concerning the location of "phrenological organs" in the brain, published in the early 1800s, was made up of twenty-six circular regions devoted in large part to "criminal" traits, such as murder and theft, but also included two separate centers for language: one for the memory of words and another for articulate speech. When his successors modified this design in favor of a map with a more geographical appearance wherein no area of the brain remained unlabeled, they changed the names of Gall's criminal regions to denote other qualities—such as "amativeness," "concentrativeness," and "adhesiveness"(!)— that better coincided with the moral and religious concerns of the day. While the beliefs of the phrenologists have been wholly discredited by modern science, the underlying concept they introduced—that specific physical structures in the brain might be linked in some fashion to ability, behavior, and personality—was a valuable idea and provided the foundation for the next (and more scientifically credible) wave of what are now called "localizationist" theories of the brain's organization for language. And they'll change, too. But at least we're making progress.

While the phrenologists incorporated evidence from disabilities following brain damage, they tended to jump to fanciful conclusions on the basis of only a few cases that supported their beliefs. Of course, this is not at all unlike what most people do every day, but such thinking is a prime example of how good evidence can be used in the wrong way. For example, it is naïve to assume, on the basis of one individual, that a function is represented in a particular brain area just because the function is disrupted after damage to that area. After all, a champion swimmer can't swim well with a broken arm, but this shouldn't lead us to conclude that swimming ability resides in the arm. So in order for aphasia evidence to be useful in forming plausible hypotheses about brain organization, large amounts of data must be amassed and closely evaluated. If a sufficiently high number of similar conditions and results are observed, only then can one make a reasonable guess about the mechanisms responsible for such results.

It wasn't until the work of Pierre Paul Broca, who reported in an 1865 paper that language loss was more commonly associated with left-brain injury than right-brain injury, that the idea of a language center came to be seriously considered and studied in the general scientific community. Broca is now considered a pioneer in the field of neuropsychology, having been the first to explicitly state that "we speak with the left hemisphere" after conducting a scientific analysis of collected observations. The area he indicated as that which controls speech—a section of the left frontal lobe—is now called "Broca's area" in his honor. Another pioneer to receive a similar honor is the German neurologist Carl Wernicke, who discovered that damage to a different part of the left hemisphere, behind and below Broca's area, had a greater effect on language comprehension than language output. "Wernicke's area" is located in the posterior temporal lobe and is thought to play a dominant role in language comprehension.

Interestingly, although Wernicke indicated that specific functions appeared to be tied to this area, and although his discovery led to a strengthening of localizational theory, his overall conception of how the brain produces higher functions actually contradicted the localizationist view in many ways. He is credited with being among the first to propose a model of the brain that controlled language not through the efforts of one general area, but through the cooperation of several different areas responsible for components of language. This view is a predecessor of sorts to the current prevailing views that envision language as the product of complex, layered networks of specialized connections in the brain. But it was not a popular view in Wernicke's time, presumably because it could not be definitively proven by the available aphasics data.

According to Harry Whitaker's account in the *Handbook of Neurolinguistics*, despite Wernicke's leanings and the occasional challenge from other proponents of the connectionist model, ". . . the localization model persevered until, by the second half of the 20th century, classical neurolinguistics became firmly entrenched in both clinical and experimental neuroscience research." The switch he describes, which finally upset the firmly entrenched localizationist view, marks the birth of modern neurolinguistics, which differs from its classical predecessor by incorporating knowledge and methods from not just the two fields indicated by its name (neurology and linguistics), but also psychology, speech pathology, cognitive science, advanced imaging technology, and artificial intelligence.

The generally heightened interest in psycholinguistics and cognitive psychology in the fifties caused an influx of new thinking that was concerned with linking ability and behavior not to anatomical structures, but to theoretical cognitive ones. It became clear through this marriage of disciplines that exclusive study of damaged brains would never yield an acceptable understanding of normal language processes and that adding research that focused on the cognitive processes of "normal" subjects would help not only to round out existing theories but to create new ones as well.

Then, the introduction and rapid sophistication of computers in recent decades allowed for the addition of three revolutionary tools: (1) new computational models of normal and abnormal language processes, which were previously limited in scope by human computational speeds; (2) the development of advanced imaging techniques such as CAT-scans, PET-scans, and MRIs, which allow researchers to observe the brain's linguistic functions in action; and (3) the use of artificial neural networks to simulate language processes in the brain.[1] (Also,

---

1. See Chapter Five of this book for more detailed descriptions of these technologies and their various contributions to brain-language research.

data obtained from these tools put to rest a popular—and unscientific—myth: the common notion that you use only 10 percent of your brain is completely wrong. You use 100 percent of it.)

The changes in neurolinguistic thought in the fifty years since its re-creation have been characterized by a movement away from the idea of language as a collection of "skills" (such as reading and writing) that originate in distinct areas of the brain to the more modular view that these skills are themselves products of complex connections between different sets of structures in the brain. Caramazza writes, "In this framework, notions like 'reading center' are meaningless, since reading is assumed to be the product of a vast network of perceptual/cognitive/motor mechanisms involving many areas of the left and right hemisphere. There is no single brain center for reading, writing, or comprehension. There are only networks of highly specific mechanisms dedicated to the individual operations that comprise a complex task." Even shopping requires your entire brain to be engaged. (Personally, I believe that certain activities require your entire brain to be *disengaged*, but I wouldn't want to enumerate them here.)

Spelling actually contains many sublevels of activity. And because spelling is one of the first things we learn in school, we might be inclined to assume that it's one of the more basic language tasks, at least in terms of activity in the brain. But this assumption would be incorrect. Ahh! At last, a little sympathy from our friendly neighborhood neuropsychologist. As Nadine Martin explains in her contribution to the *Handbook of Neurolinguistics* entitled "Recovery and Treatment of Acquired Reading and Spelling Disorders," ". . . writing is not simply the reverse of reading in the same way that speaking is not simply the reverse of hearing and comprehending . . .

the pathways to spelling vary depending on the task. Writing thoughts to compose a letter involves a different combination of processes than writing a dictated letter or copying lecture notes from a chalkboard."

Q & A WITH NADINE MARTIN

Nadine Martin is Associate Research Scientist at the Center for Cognitive Neuroscience at Temple University in Philadelphia, Pennsylvania.

MvS: *What has the study of spelling disorders contributed to our understanding of how normal spelling is accomplished in the brain?*

NM: By analyzing the kinds of errors that occur in spelling (that is, omissions of letters, transpositions, phonic spelling of irregularly spelled words, and so on), we are able to infer what psycholinguistic stages of the spelling process are affected. These sorts of data confirm theories of how spelling processes work.

MvS: *Has any research with which you're familiar indicated whether the neurological "wiring" of a bad speller differs from that of a good speller?*

NM: There are undoubtedly differences, just as there are differences that somehow lead to an exceptional musical ability or some other talent. But "difference" is the key word: not deficit.

MvS: *In English-speaking cultures, bad spelling tends to lead to negative assumptions about the writer's intelligence, despite psycholinguistic evidence indicating that one cannot reliably predict the other and that spelling ability and performance may be linked more closely to our senses and emotions. What, in your opinion, might the current understanding of spelling processes in the brain contribute to this discussion?*

NM: It is important to view spelling as a function that is not necessary to human function, but is functionally useful in today's world. Spelling disorders may be perceived as a handicap, but only in view of the fact that spelling is useful in today's world. There are different reading and spelling cognitive styles: some individuals read phonically, some visually, and some a combination of both. The latter sort allows ample ability in sounding out new words and recognizing irregularly spelled words that cannot be sounded out. The important thing to remember with spelling disorders is that they often reflect a cognitive style that may not work in all situations. . . . The combination of basic cognitive processes varies across individuals—we all have these abilities, but they are not qualitatively uniform in each individual. Behaviors such as spelling and reading emerge from unique combinations of fundamental abilities in each individual. In and of itself, spelling is not a measure of the intelligence of an individual.

New insights into the brain's mechanisms for spelling tell us more than just how our brains allow us to spell. Because spelling is inherent in all our interactions with language, its networks and pathways are microcosms of those in the larger language system. So, in essence, what we learn about spelling, we learn about brain language as a whole. In addition, each new revelation about a specific brain function informs what we already know—or think we know—about how the brain works in general and moves us that much closer to our goal of a true and productive understanding of this most fabulous and mysterious of human possessions.

Marcus E. Raichle, in a 1994 article for *Scientific American*, compares the mechanisms of the brain to an orchestra and the various functions it performs to a symphony: ". . . networks of neurons residing in strictly localized areas perform thought processes. So just as specific members of a large orchestra perform together in a precise fashion to produce a symphony, a group of localized brain areas performing elementary operations work together to exhibit an observable human behavior." We can only hope to gain enough insight into the workings of the brain that we eventually become conductors of this orchestra and not just members of the awestruck audience.

CHAPTER 4

THE SPELLING POLICE:
Who Makes Up These Rules, Anyway?

There are no rules in English; only exceptions.
—as related by ROGER MITTON,
British author

Asking who is responsible for the complexities of the English spelling system is like asking who invented music. The answer to both questions is: no one and everyone. (But unlike music, if there *were* someone responsible for the English spelling system, he or she would surely never admit it.) The English language, like music, has always been a mirror of culture, so as the norms of English society changed and grew more convoluted—an understatement, right?—the standards of its language did the same. This happens with every language, of course, but because early English culture acted as a crossroads for so many other well-developed languages and cultures and underwent, as a result, frequent and numerous transformations, the effect is more dramatic.

In the preface to his 1927 book *English Spelling: Its Rules and Reasons*, W. A. Craigie suggests that the chaotic appearance of the English spelling system is a mistaken impression due to the lack of an organized presentation. He explains: "The first step towards correcting that impression is to obtain a clear idea of the reasons for the variety in the forms, and of the sources from which they are usually derived. It will then be seen that most of the peculiarities have a historical basis, and to that extent are legitimate, however much they may be in opposition to each other and to the pronunciation of the present day." So at least we have an excuse.

But you could argue that written English, like good jazz and great opera, was encumbered by complexity from the start. A very brief history of the language will be helpful: The first *spoken* form of what we now call English was the dialect spoken by the German settlers (now referred to as the Anglo-Saxons, after two of the three main tribes—the Angles, Saxons, and Jutes—of which the settling population was composed) who took over Britain in the fifth century A.D. But the first *written* form to which our English orthography can be traced came a full century later, when Roman and Irish missionaries converted the Anglo-Saxons to Christianity and introduced them to the Roman alphabet.[1] And so that excuse is:

---

1. The Anglo-Saxons were familiar with writing before the introduction of Christianity and used a runic alphabet to record the spoken

English orthography began not as a result of a natural and parallel evolution of characters and sounds, but as a marriage of two separately developed forms.

Try committing just that one above paragraph to memory, and if your employer ever calls you on the carpet because of your spelling, you'll have an impressive reply and a splendid defense.

Roger Mitton remarks on the artificial nature of English orthography in *English Spelling and the Computer*: ". . . the Roman alphabet, of course, was devised for representing a different language. Any linguist devising an alphabet for English from scratch would devise one with more letters, especially for vowel sounds, but we are stuck with the Roman ones." Indeed, this pairing did result in our having perhaps too many options for consonant sounds and not enough for vowel sounds, which is presumably what prompted George Henry Vallins to write in his book, *Spelling*, that ". . . paradoxically the English alphabet is at once inadequate and embarrassingly rich."

The word embarrassing seems especially apt, at least as far as spelling is concerned. Written English, even at its inception, was never as easy to learn and understand as the written languages that had more direct ties between letters and sounds, such as Italian, Finnish, and Serbo-Croatian. These languages are commonly understood to have "shallow" alphabets, a concept explained by Philip H. K. Seymour: If the relationship between the speech elements and the written symbols is reliable and consistent, knowl-

---

language, evidence of which is found in the several non-Roman characters used alongside Roman ones in writings from the written language's first few hundred years, but as these functioned only as supplements to the Roman system and eventually died out, it's fair to say that the Roman alphabet was directly and completely superimposed onto the existing spoken language. In any case, it is certain that the Roman alphabet was not native to English and that thus the pairing was inherently artificial and awkward.

edge of the sound-symbol pairings is sufficient for the correct spelling of any word in the language. This is the reason that such languages are much easier for both native
and non-native users to spell and pronounce than English
has ever been. The last time I was in Italy, I noticed that
although I didn't know what many of the items on the
menu were, I had no problem ordering them perfectly!

Despite its shortcomings, the original English alphabet prevailed, thanks to the efforts of the church. (Or
perhaps blame is in order.) English writing spread along
with the Christian message to monasteries throughout
England, where it was taught to the scribes who copied
religious manuscripts. But there were no specific conventions governing how each word was to be spelled.
Within the phonetic possibilities, "a scribe's spelling of a
particular word depended partly on the local conventions, partly on his dialect and partly on choice—he
might spell the same word in different ways in the same
manuscript," writes Mitton. And I know plenty of people
who do the same thing today!

But over the next three hundred years, the large number of books in circulation decreased the number of local
dialects and promoted in particular the prominence of a
dialect native to West Saxon, which, during a newly vigor-
ous attempt to unify monastic efforts in the mid-tenth
century, became established as the standard form. This
period of unification is singled out by linguists as the high
point for English spelling in terms of phoneme/grapheme
correspondence: that is, the spelling and pronunciation of
words conformed more closely at this time than at any
other. So, what happened?

Once the orthography became stable, it fell out of
step with the pronunciation almost immediately.
Pronunciation changes throughout the first half of the
eleventh century obscured the sound/spelling relation-

ship and began to effect local dissension from the previous spelling standard. But these changes were minor
compared to what happened next: war.

Of all the changes for which war is blamed, I'll bet
you never thought of *spelling*. Yet in 1066, the Norman
Conquest brought large numbers of French-speaking settlers to England, and as these settlers had no knowledge
of (or use for) English, the French language—after two
centuries of existing alongside English as a second living
language—became the language of the ruling class
throughout the country and thus the preferred language
for all bureaucratic written discourse (religious and other
written discourse reverted to Latin) and remained so
until the fourteenth century.

Then things got even worse. The influx of French and
a renewed interest in Latin caused confusion for the few
scribes that did maintain their English writing skills,
which resulted in many spelling changes based on
French constructions that survive to this day, such as
"queen," which was originally spelled *cwen*, and "what,"
previously spelled *hwaet*. And in general, this confusion
further weakened any notions of a uniform spelling
standard for the language because there was no longer
any central authority even to dictate one. Donald Scragg,
in *A History of English Spelling*, cites a particularly striking
example of the lax attitude toward spelling, pointing out
a thirteenth-century manuscript in which a scribe apparently lost his place in the copy text and accidentally
copied the same section of text twice. The surprising
result is that seven of the words in this short passage are
spelled differently the second time around.

Q & A WITH DONALD SCRAGG

Donald Scragg is Professor of Anglo-Saxon Studies at the University of Manchester and the author of *A History of English Spelling*. He is also President of the Simplified Spelling Society, an organization that has promoted English spelling reform since 1908.

MvS: *The biggest role in the spelling history saga seems to have belonged to the scribes, but the nature of that role is complicated: They were clearly a strong force for stabilization, but at the same time, they were responsible for introducing many inconsistencies into the mix, due to their various backgrounds, dialects, and personal agendas. Would you say that the overall contribution of the scribes was more positive or negative?*

DS: Scribes, like the compositors of printed material that followed them, were professionals, and their work would be of use only if they could communicate effectively and efficiently with their readers. This is the test that should be applied to them, not how history (that is, we) would judge them, according to *our* agendas. Those more truly responsible for stabilizing English spelling are not those who, in your words, were responsible for introducing many inconsistencies into the mix, but those who chose an individual spelling from the variants available for each word. And these are the makers of the spelling books and early dictionaries of the late sixteenth and early seventeenth centuries. If you want someone to "blame" for inconsistencies in current practice, try sixteenth-century schoolmasters who inculcated spelling in their pupils.

MvS: *Do you think that the increasing ubiquity of the English language will help or hurt the current spelling standards?*

DS: English is a world language because of (first of all) British and (now) American cultural and commercial imperialism, not to put too fine a point on it. I doubt if there will be any greater impact on spelling in the twenty-first century from this fact than there was in the nineteenth or twentieth century. What may prove more important is the electronic revolution, with spelling-checkers in every household PC.

But it is worth noting that not until relatively recently has written language been regarded as an important expression of language in its own right, having separate qualities and uses that are not provided by spoken expression. Written language, and particularly written English during this period, was seen only as a means of recording the "real" language, which was the spoken one. Great literature would have to wait. Not until English writing came to be rigorously standardized and used for purposes other than religious, legal, or official ones, did it come to be understood as an entity that is in many ways separate from its spoken counterpart.

Throughout this French-dominated period, English writing actually died out among the scribes; it was no longer being taught but was at least maintained regionally by independent religious leaders and their followers, for whom English was the vernacular. The permanent revival of a uniform orthography for English didn't occur until a capital was established in London in the fifteenth century. When political power shifted to that central location, large numbers of important legal documents sharing the same London standard began to be circulated nationwide, and this standard that the Chancery scribes eventually settled on has lasted, in large part, to the present day. Had the capital been located somewhere other than London, our spelling today would most probably be quite different, as Scragg points out: "If the ambulatory kings of the Middle Ages had settled in Hereford or Worcester, or even in Gloucester where they frequently held court, the antecedent of the modern spelling system would probably have been not unlike the AB language.[2] If Oxford, another

2. Here is Scragg's explanation of the AB language: "Two manuscripts are central to the study of . . . West Midlands prose: Corpus

favourite royal centre, had been chosen, then modern
spelling might have developed from the Wycliffite literary
standard. But the court settled in London, and as the capital grew in size, in administrative importance, and in
wealth, the language spoken and, more particularly, written there increased in authority."

What becomes clear from studying the history of
English spelling is that the most influential moments
have been the results of decisive rather than inventive
acts. Where we've attempted to remodel the system by
introducing new forms, we've almost always failed. What
this means to us today is that the most effective way of
furthering a language and the culture it defines is not by
attempting to reinvent it—which essentially means starting from scratch and thus moving backward—but instead
promoting its organization and precision, which enriches
its use and urges it forward. The years from 1400 to 1600
were arguably the most dramatic for English spelling
because in that two-century span, three influential events
occurred: the Great Vowel Shift, which still torments us
today; the birth and flowering of the Renaissance, which
brought a renewed interest in the civilizations of classical
Greece and Rome and thus an influx of Greek and Latin
words and spellings; and the stabilization of spelling as a
result of the printing press.

The remarkable phenomenon now known as the
Great Vowel Shift occurred in London and then
throughout England from 1400 to 1600 as a result of the

Christi College, Cambridge, MS 402, containing a version of the
text called *Ancrene Wisse* ('Anchoresses' knowledge'), and Bodlein
library MS Bodley 34, containing the saints' lives. . . . The two manuscripts, written by different scribes and containing material very
distinct in kind and quality, have a unique importance in early
Middle English in that they employ an identical system of spelling
and accidence. Their written dialect is known to philologists as the
AB language, 'A' for *Ancrene Wisse* and 'B' for Bodley 34."

streams of young immigrants entering the capital and introducing disparate dialects into the speech. This had a profound effect on the relationship of spelling to sound in many English words. During this period, all long vowels came to be pronounced with the jaw position one degree higher, except for the two highest vowels, which became diphthongs (complex sounds that begin with one vowel and end in another, such as the "oi" sound in "boil."). This transformation caused "ay" sounds to switch to "ee," and "ee" sounds to switch to "I" (as in pie). For example, "deed" before the shift rhymed with our current pronunciation of "maid," and "life" rhymed with our current pronunciation of "leaf." Unfortunately, this revolution of pronunciation overlapped with a widespread movement toward stabilization in spelling, so many spellings that made phonetic sense before the shift remained unchanged afterward and became miserably awkward! As Roger Mitton says, "Though there are advantages in having a stable orthography, it is unfortunate that the fixing took place when it did—roughly between 1550 and 1650. Another hundred years of confusion might have allowed some of the more awkward Latinate respellings to disappear ('debt,' 'receipt,' and the like) and it would also have allowed spellings to adjust to modern pronunciation." In other words, Mitton is stating that in the case of English, a hundred more years of confusion would have *helped*!

The printing press, which eventually played a large role in stabilizing English spelling for good, initially caused more confusion than it allayed because the standards of each printing house were influenced by different dialects; also, printers would use whichever spelling helped align the text the best. (This topic is discussed at greater length in Chapter Five.) But by 1650, the general movement toward a stable and unified system, com-

bined with the permanence and reach of printing technology, caused the spellings that happened to be currently in use to be "flash-frozen," inconsistencies and all.
"Simply because many copies of a given work could
exist," writes Mitton, "many people could share the
same standard. The spellings of the established printing
houses were codified and taught to schoolchildren; the
children would grow up to expect the same spellings in
their reading matter, and the printers would be careful to
stick to them. There was no place for innovation in this
cycle, and the argument for conservatism grew stronger
as the mountain of material in print grew ever larger."

The introduction of paper had made book production
cheaper and started a movement away from public recitation—which had been necessitated by a scarcity of books
and low literacy levels in the general population—and
toward reading as a private activity. This transition was
completed by the printing press, which made book production both cheap and fast. And as private reading
became more common and literacy levels rose, the inconsistencies of the spelling system became more widely
apparent, and people began to speak out against them.

Thus began in earnest the long tradition, still ongoing,
of calling for English spelling reform[3] and, concurrently,
the more widespread discussion of the need for an

3. However, the earliest remaining example of spelling reform is
from much earlier, in a manuscript from around 1200 entitled
Ormulum after its author, known only as Orm. The orthography in
this work is wholly original and highly consistent. It had no effect
on modern spelling reform but is considered important because it
serves as an invaluable guide to medieval pronunciation and
because, according to George Henry Vallins, ". . . Orm recognised
the two principles that underlie the proposals of all reformers who
have followed him: that consistency, and the perfect correspondence of sound and symbol—that is, the use of one symbol to represent one sound, and one sound only—were the chief necessities."

English dictionary. According to Donald Scragg, the reform controversy officially began with "a prominent Cambridge don, Sir Thomas Smith, producing the first detailed argument in favor of orthographic consistency in a book printed in 1568." Interestingly, this book, entitled *De recta and emendata linguae anglicae scriptione, dialogus*[4] was written in Latin and not in the language with which it took issue. A possible explanation for this is offered by Gerry Knowles in *A Cultural History of the English Language*: "The fact that he published in Paris a book written in Latin suggests that he was writing essentially for the international scholarly readership and that his aim was of a theoretical and linguistic nature. If he had really wanted to influence spelling practice he would surely have written in English." Then again, maybe he just didn't want his book to be full of spelling errors.

The first significant document of this kind written in English was a book known as *The Elementarie*, written by a schoolmaster named Richard Mulcaster in 1582. While plenty of English-Latin and English-French translation dictionaries had been produced, not until Mulcaster's lifetime had anyone felt a need for an "English-English" dictionary meant exclusively for *native* users of the language. But many of Mulcaster's contemporaries did, and Mulcaster himself set forth in *The Elementarie* an argument for gathering together and categorizing all English words, accompanied by a list of recommended spellings for around eight thousand of them. None of these spellings were new: they were simply the ones Mulcaster chose from the current varieties as being the most logical. While Mulcaster was an advocate of spelling reform, his opinions on appropriate methods differed from those

4. "Dialogue concerning the correct and amended writing of the English language."

of his contemporaries in that he rejected the idea of a purely phonetic system and saw value in, as Knowles puts it, "reason and custom." The words were not defined because the focus was on orthography specifically. Nevertheless, the book is now seen as one of the few significant precursors to the first actual dictionary of English and is credited by Scragg as the crucial first step toward spelling stabilization: ". . . the stabilisation of English orthography owes more to *The Elementarie* than to all the efforts of those who wished to reform the orthography on scientific lines."

At the time, *The Elementarie* did not garner much attention beyond the bounds of academia—it was aimed at other schoolmasters and language scholars—but its sentiments (and a large part of its word list) were carried on in 1596 by a much more accessible book, *The Englishe Schoole-maister*, written by another schoolmaster named Edmund Coote. Although Coote's book had similar aims to Mulcaster's—namely, to be a teaching aid—it consciously appealed to people of all walks of life: "people without Latin . . . and such men and women of trades (as Taylors, Weavers, Shop-keepers, Seamsters, and such other) as haue vndertaken the charge of teaching others." As a result of its broad appeal and the apparent need and desire at the time for a shared spelling standard, the book enjoyed nearly unprecedented success, running to over forty editions and remaining in print until the early eighteenth century. The fact that Coote, unlike Mulcaster, included synonyms for the words in his list, prompts Jonathan Green, in *Chasing the Sun*, to credit him with producing ". . . in effect a prototype 'modern' dictionary." (Imagine: a dictionary hitting the best-seller list!)

But according to most scholars, Green included, the first book worthy of the descriptor "dictionary" for the English language is Robert Cawdrey's 1604 *A Table*

Alphabeticall. What distinguishes Cawdrey's work from its predecessors is that it was the first purely English list of words and definitions to be issued as an independent work. Although the term "lexicographer" is not documented as having entered the English language until 1658—as a combination of the Greek words *lexicon*, dictionary, and *graphos*, writing or a writer (Green)— Cawdrey was most certainly one. Like Coote, he "borrowed" material from his predecessors, adopting almost 90 percent of the *Table*'s word list and adding to that material from a Latin-English dictionary by Thomas Thomas. His third major source is a subject of some interest and amusement now because it was so full of anomalous words and spellings: a translation from Latin to English of Oswald Gabelkhouer's medical work, *The Boock of Physicke*, by a Dutchman known only as "A.M." who had all but forgotten his English and in many places throughout the text merely put English endings on Latin words. Having been alerted to this problem before publication, A.M. inserted a glossary of these words, offering by way of definition what he hoped would be more readily understandable synonyms. It is this glossary that Cawdrey drew from, and the result is that a third of the terms in *Table Alphabeticall* were essentially gibberish (for example: *puluerisated*, meaning "beaten," *frigifye*, meaning "to cool," *calefye*, meaning "to heat," and *ebulliated*, meaning "boiled") but nonetheless became legitimized (at least temporarily) by their inclusion in such an important work.

Over the next hundred years, many instructional spelling books inspired by Coote came to be published and used in schools, as did increasingly elaborate dictionaries, following, for the most part, the pattern set down by Cawdrey. As spelling became entrenched as a subject of study in schools, there began to be a clear disparity between educated and uneducated spelling. "It became possible," notes Mitton, "to judge the level of someone's education, in a rough and ready way, by looking at their spelling, whence the long history of mockery which poor spellers have had to endure." (In this case, times *don't* change, do they?) Mitton goes on to point out that women, who were generally ill-educated at the time, were particularly persecuted as a result of this stigma and became the subjects of many a joke. Interestingly, however, women seem to have had their "revenge" in the end, evidenced by the numerous studies indicating that they now tend to be better spellers than men.[5]

By the late eighteenth century, a general atmosphere of social "refinement" and "purification" through conformity to certain ideals had permeated English culture, and this was, of course, represented closely in prevailing attitudes toward language. Rumblings among the learned members of society about the need to codify the language through an authoritative and comprehensive written work grew louder and more insistent, inspiring several concerted attempts, which would ultimately fail from lack of funds or resolve. Ultimately, it was the poet Samuel Johnson's *Dictionary of the English Language* of 1755 that rose to the task and succeeded, although the spellings it offered were, on the whole, less radical than many that were being proposed. Johnson was as unhappy as anyone with the inconsistencies in spelling but became increas-

5. David Moseley, in the *Handbook of Spelling*, says, "Many more boys than girls have problems with spelling and with punctuation (Moseley, 1972, 1974). In a population of 1254 8–9-year-olds in 16 schools there were twice as many boys as girls with spelling quotients of 75 or less, and among those with average or above scores on the English Picture Vocabulary Test (Brimer & Dunn, 1962) five times as many boys as girls were poor spellers."

ingly aware, while compiling the more than forty-three thousand words that composed his dictionary, that drastic reform would be not only a Herculean task, but also futile in the end, maintaining that "language is the work of man, of a being from whom permanence and stability cannot be derived." Nonetheless, Johnson was authoritative in his choices, and, as Mitton says, "Dr. Johnson's dictionary was perhaps the final nail that pinned the orthography down; everyone could now use the same authoritative work of reference, whether for private writing or for publication." (It sounds more like the final nail in the coffin, doesn't it?) Knowles writes, "The spelling of the vast majority of English words was fixed in 1755; apart from the simplification of the final <ck> in *musick*, and the American innovations, there have been no systematic changes in spelling."

The permanence of Johnson's spellings is often attributed in part to a prevailing attitude at the time, which persists today, that the standard form of a language is the "correct" form and that all others are inferior to it and somehow corrupt. Knowles states clearly the argument against this idea: "The confusion of 'standard' with 'correct' created a new kind of standard, a standard of acceptability which most people would in one way or another fail to achieve. This is in its nature socially divisive. . . . People's literacy skills, their command of English, their social class and even their intelligence have come to be routinely measured according to the degree to which they conform to the arbitrary conventions of usage." The meanings with which certain spellings are imbued even today is exemplified in a statement made by Gore Vidal in a 1992 *Time* magazine interview: "Ultimately it's all a matter of style. What it comes down to is this: Do you spell Jennifer with a J or G? That's a class division. As a populist, I'm all for G."

Funny: I thought it was a matter of what your parents decided to have printed on your birth certificate!

The authority of the spelling standards established by Johnson was strong enough to withstand the journey across the Atlantic to America where, despite a good amount of strong sentiment to the contrary, a large majority of the spellings have been maintained to this day. Such linguistic loyalty is surprising, considering the circumstances of the colonists' leave-taking and the great distance that lay between them and their language's point of origin, but it was due in large part to the sheer volume of printed matter and the extent to which the colonists were already accustomed to reading and writing the language in a certain way. In sum: it could have been even worse than it is. Keep this in mind the next time you celebrate Thanksgiving. You have even *more* to celebrate.

All this is not to say that there weren't repeated, organized attempts at change, for indeed there were many, and chief among them—in terms of effectiveness and notoriety—were those of Noah Webster. Webster, born in Connecticut three years after the first publication of the Johnson dictionary, was a teacher for many years before starting his own school, and it was his frustration with the deficiencies of current textbooks and their negative effects on his students' language skills that inspired him to come up with a book of his own: *A Grammatical Institute of the English Language*, which contained sections on spelling, grammar, and reading. While the grammar and reading material had no great lasting success, the spelling section was so popular that it merited republishing on its own in 1788, which met with astonishing success. Green characterizes it as ". . . one of the greatest publishing success stories of the century, going on to be one of the best-selling, if not the best-selling nonfiction work in America, rivaled only by the Bible." (Further imagine: a book about *spelling* hitting the best-seller list. Why, my imagination is hereby exhausted.) The book, which came to be popularly known as the "Blue-Back Speller" quickly became a staple in schools and homes to the extent that a new term, *Websterian*, was coined in his honor.

The surprising thing about this speller, though, is that it borrows largely from the Johnson dictionary, as Webster had not yet begun to champion the revolutionary ideas about spelling for which he later became so (in)famous; at the time, he considered Johnson to be, in his words, "the most approved authority in the language." Not long after the speller's completion, however, he began corresponding with Benjamin Franklin, who had written a book twenty years prior entitled *Scheme for a New Alphabet and a Reformed Mode of Spelling*, which proposed a radically different spelling system that incorporated a whole new alphabet and was designed to better represent the sounds of the language. While the specific plan Franklin proposed seemed impractical to Webster, he agreed with the general sentiment behind it and began designing his own spelling reform: a pattern of simplification for many words based on eliminating "silent" letters, which he deemed superfluous. An example of a proposed change that became accepted as an American spelling is the elimination of the *u* in "colour."

His proposal was highly controversial, contradicting as it did the Johnsonian standard, and thus, the established standard of England. And Webster was not only aware of the political implications of his proposal but in fact championed them as the key reason for implementing the plan. This raised the question of whether his aims were now more focused on improving the orthography or on severing ties to England and creating a

uniquely American form of English. The argument
Webster presents in *Dissertations on the English Language*
seems to leave no doubt regarding his primary agenda:

> A capital advantage of this reform in these States would be
> that it would make a difference between the English orthog-
> raphy and the American. This will startle those who have
> not attended to the subject; but I am confident that such an
> event is an object of vast political consequence. The alter-
> ation, however small, would encourage the publication of
> books in our own country. It would render it, in some meas-
> ure, necessary that all books should be printed in America.
> The English would never copy our orthography for their
> own use; and consequently the same impressions of books
> would not answer for both countries. The inhabitants of the
> present generation would read the English impressions; but
> posterity, being taught a different spelling, would prefer the
> American orthography.

Webster's main legacy, of course, is not having
reformed English spelling, although he effected several
lasting changes, but having created the first successful
English dictionary to include "Americanisms." While
spelling remained relatively fixed, pronunciation and
usage had fluctuated greatly since the colonization, and
his first as well as succeeding dictionaries documented
these fluctuations. Hugh Kenner, in his article for the
National Review entitled "On American Words," points
out that while England and America may share the same
concern for upholding the standards of their common
language, they show it in altogether different ways:
"Still, however necessary attention to spelling may be, it
needn't entail rituals the like of spelling bees. There's a
story, documented, about folk in—was it Nebraska?—
whose nineteenth-century ritual was to circulate weekend by weekend to one another's parlors for an evening
of, yes, spelling. Imagine that in Sussex! No, it seems
specifically North American."

Not all the early American reformers based their arguments on political grounds, especially because in time,
independence seemed more secure and an American
identity appeared to be duly establishing itself. Most
arguments for reform have centered around the disparity
between pronunciation and spelling and the fact that
this creates an obstacle to learning that users of the language should not have to overcome. Scragg's characteri-
zation of the sentiment of Webster's successors in reform
is also applicable to those of today: ". . . the principal
concern was over the waste of energy and expense
involved in the teaching of spelling."

By 1900, there were several large, well-funded organizations for spelling reform in England and America, and
many prominent figures of the day—literary, political,
and otherwise—were contributing to the discussion. One
such notable contributor was the dramatist George
Bernard Shaw, who objected to the established spelling
system on the grounds that it was a waste of a writer's
time and energy and, in characteristic fashion, designed
his own original alphabet, instructions for the use of
which he set forth in great detail in his will. Despite
these measures, his proposed changes, not surprisingly,
were never adopted.

One interesting development that took place during
this period, though—and did have a permanent effect
on the orthography—was the government-led stabilization of American geographical spellings. Until 1890,
when the U.S. Board on Geographic Names was established, many American place names had been variously
spelled because, as Richard Venezky points out in *The
American Way of Spelling*, "Many . . . were transliterated
from languages that either had no writing systems or
were written with non-roman letters." Place names
derived from Native American words, especially, but also

those that originated in family names and biblical and mythological sources, had fallen through the cracks of the otherwise well-stabilized American orthography because there had been no central authority to regulate them. One of the examples provided by Venezky is the spelling of the name "Wisconsin," which, for the first two hundred years (from the time the area was first explored by French settlers), was spelled at least three different ways—*Ouisconsin*, *Wiskonsin*, and *Wisconsan*— and probably more. Some changes made by the Board were later reversed—such as the removal of the *h* from *Pittsburgh*—but its influence was in large part effective. The considerable efforts of several American newspapers throughout the early 1900s to simplify certain well-known unphonetic spellings met a different fate: they were ultimately defeated by public outcry at the unfamiliar new forms.

Q & A WITH RICHARD VENEZKY

Richard Venezky is Unidel Professor of Educational Studies at the University of Delaware, and Research Director of the ICT Program of the Organization for Economic Co-operation and Development in Paris. He is the author most recently of *The American Way of Spelling: The Structure and Origins of American English Orthography.*

MvS: *You note in the epilogue to the reform chapter of your latest book that it is the nature of society to resist rapid changes not only in spelling, but in phonology, syntax, and vocabulary as well. To what, then, do you attribute the phenomenon known as "The Great Vowel Shift"? It was a dramatic moment in the history of the language, yet there seem to be no formal theories as to its causes. Do you have any theories about it? Granted, pronunciation changes a bit with each new generation, but what could have been the motivating forces behind such an unusually drastic (and strangely pervasive) change?*

RV: Sound change occurs in all languages over time; however, there is little understanding of what initiates and what provides the continuing pressure for particular changes. Some linguists speculate that contact with another language or dialect sometimes creates an unconscious drive either to emulate the sounds of the contact language or dialect, if it is spoken by a group with higher prestige, or to differentiate ones own pronunciation further from it if it is spoken by people with lower prestige. Wilder speculations center on climatic change, leading to subtle changes in the physiology of speech, and changes in social relationships, leading to the desire of some groups to differentiate themselves from other groups in the same society.

MvS: *What conclusions do you draw from history regarding the possibility and necessity of English spelling reform today? That is, do you think history shows that reform is impossible, or just that the methods employed thus far have been ill-conceived? And as a related but separate question, do you believe a reform of our current spelling system is necessary?*

RV: The primary conclusion I draw from the history of the English language, and especially the history of the politics of the English language, is that spelling reform, for all its logical appeal, has had and continues to have minimal support from those who could most easily direct its change: educators, lexicographers, literary leaders, and publishers. A major part of the lack of appeal has been the manner in which spelling reform has been approached in the past. The claims that we lose one to two years of education because of spelling irregularities or that international business is hampered by the same cause are quite hollow and are rarely bolstered by any empirical evidence. Limited spelling reform remains possible and desirable, nevertheless, but primarily through gradual change. Spellings such as thru, tho, and thoro need to be established first as acceptable alternatives in schooling, legal documents, and the like.

The American Federation of Teachers, the National Education Association, and their British, Canadian, and Australian counterparts need to be convinced that backing such an effort is within their own interests. Similarly, major presses (Oxford, Cambridge, University of Chicago) need to be recruited. The alternative route is to promote spelling reform as a grassroots campaign on the Internet, but this risks reinforcing a growing perception that e-mail and the World Wide Web are encouraging sloppy, if not barbarous writing habits. This, in turn, could create a highly conservative countermovement in the schools, restoring sentence-diagramming, memorization of spelling rules and definitions of parts of speech, and meaningless drill on correct spellings.

MvS: *How, in your opinion, can an awareness of spelling history help a native speaker improve his or her spelling?*

RV: Learning to spell requires, in part, learning the peculiarities and irregularities of hundreds of words. Knowledge of the history of English spelling can provide the frameworks needed to retain much of this information, as well as the sensitivity to suspect that with many words, spelling will not be totally regular. In some cases, the facilitation is no more than the association of words that have similar spelling anomalies (could, would, should; debt, doubt, subtle; and so on) and similar histories; in other cases, it's knowing that a particular sound change was not accompanied by a corresponding spelling change (for example, write, wrong, wrap, wreck). This same history can also help with the pronunciation of words from their spellings, but in both cases many other factors need to be considered. The strongest reason for learning the history of English spelling is that, like any history, it enriches our understanding of the past, it makes us more adept at causal reasoning, and it sensitizes us to the richness of the current orthography.

William Strunk, Jr., in his classic writing guide, *The Elements of Style*, presents his explanation for the negative responses readers have to unfamiliar spellings: "The practical objection to unaccepted and oversimplified spellings is the disfavor with which they are received by the reader. They distract his attention and exhaust his patience. He reads the form *though* automatically, without thought of its needless complexity; he reads the abbreviation *tho* and mentally supplies the missing letters, at the cost of a fraction of his attention. The writer has defeated his own purpose." Roger Mitton addresses this problem as well, saying, "whatever advantages we gain by departing from the alphabetic principle, it is when we are reading, rather than writing, that we feel the benefit. When writing, most of us would surely be happier with a more alphabetic system."

Both statements suggest that the reader and the writer are at cross-purposes with each other, with the writer tending toward phonetic representation and the reader toward the etymological and familiar. But, ultimately, both reader and writer have the same goal: to free the flow of thought from its impediments. The writer wants ideas to glide smoothly from the mind to the page, and the reader wants ideas to glide smoothly from the page to the mind. The only plausible means to satisfy both seems to be an agreement upon the idea's mode of travel: a shared system that becomes so familiar to both writer and reader as to be second nature. Once this is achieved, there are no more obstacles, and the design of the standard and its underlying construction become irrelevant in the face of its flawless function. By that criteria, our English language is a spectacular success.

CHAPTER 5

SPELLING AND TECHNOLOGY:
A Love/Hate Relationship

> English spelling can seam like a maize,
> And put won strait into a hays,
> Butt now never fear,
> The spell-checker is hear,
> And its sew well-deserving of prays.
> Butt let awl pore spellers bee ware
> Of the checker and ewes it with care,
> Lest yore hair be turned into a hare.
> —Anonymous

The electronic spell-checker is only the most recent way in which technology has influenced spelling standards, and as the above poem indicates, its influence has not always been so good. In fact, almost every technological milestone to interact with spelling has had both positive and negative (or maybe it's more accurate to call them organizing and disorganizing) effects on spelling standards. Because of the quiet advent and subsequent explosion of computers and computer-related technology in the last half of this century, the word "technology" has become almost synonymous with digital communication, but while the digital revolution has had, and continues to have, many influences on the state of English spelling, the structure—and indeed the very existence—of the system we know today is due in large part to much earlier technology, a fascinating story in itself.

The birth of alphabetic writing was itself the result of technological innovation, springing as it did from a new application of one of the world's oldest tools—the stick. Western writing is commonly traced back to the Sumerians of 3100 B.C., inhabitants of southern Mesopotamia who went from using unmarked clay tokens as records for bookkeeping to inscribing these tokens with insignias that described the transactions in more detail using a reed stylus or stick on the wet clay. Eventually the Sumerians did away with the tokens altogether and used inscriptions on clay tablets to keep increasingly more detailed records of transactions. (In other words, we can credit the Sumerians with the earliest-known "paperless office.")

English writing, along with every other Western writing system, is understood to trace its beginnings from this development. But English spelling's direct relationship to technology didn't begin until centuries later, when the Roman alphabet was introduced, by means of Christianity, to the Anglo-Saxons. Previously (since about the second century A.D.), the Anglo-Saxons had used runes—simple, straight-lined characters that were well-suited to short inscriptions and meant to imbue sacred or otherwise valuable objects with greater personal meaning or to assign ownership—but neither the design of the alphabet nor the method of writing was suited to longer, more complicated written expression.

In contrast to the static nature of the runes and the laborious method of writing them, the system introduced by Roman and Irish missionaries at the end of the sixth century—a more modular, phonetic alphabet combined with the more receptive writing surfaces of parchment and vellum—was more fluid and facile, and thus more capable of approximating the organic, ongoing nature of speech. The switch from inscription to manuscripts marks the birth of what Gerry Knowles calls "a new literacy culture" for the Anglo-Saxons, in that it provided a framework for developing written forms to represent all the sounds of spoken English. This was done by borrowing the sound-letter correspondences of Latin, but where English sounds had no counterpart in Latin, creative solutions—and I do mean creative—were necessary. These solutions involved supplementing the Latin set of letters with runic characters and using digraphs (pairs of letters representing a single speech sound) to represent the non-Latin sounds. A new alphabet allowed for the existence of a spelling system and, with centuries of repetition, the emergence of several consistent patterns of spelling, with each kingdom using its own more or less (emphasis on less) cohesive style.

Awareness of the processes involved in producing this new written form of English and the creative thinking it required, reminds us of the broader meaning of the word "technology"—in fact its true definition—which is simply: "the application of knowledge to practical purposes." This underscores the fact that writing and spelling are technological achievements in and of themselves.

The next technological milestone to affect English spelling was the advent and spread of printing during the first half of the seventeenth century. "During those fifty years writers and printers, and probably the printers more than the writers," writes Craigie, "were gradually reducing to uniformity the varied orthography of the sixteenth century, which in so many words left ample scope for a choice between different forms according to the habits, taste, or learning of author, scribe or printer. With the printer the tendency towards uniformity had no doubt in some degree a physical reason; with continuous practice it became more and more natural for the compositor's hand to go to the same compartments of his case in setting up the same words, instead of hesitating between two or three alternatives." (And this is yet another reason for learning how to spell well. The constant hesitation—not to mention occasional agony—over which spelling is correct is both time-consuming and intellectually tiring.)

But although the stabilization of English spelling is owed, in large part, to the introduction of printing technology, the effect was neither straightforward nor quick. In fact, the initial effect of printing on the orthography was one of destabilization and fragmentation. While the standards of professional scribes had become fairly consistent by the early fifteenth century, and the adoption of English as the language of the Chancery scribes gave these standards good authority, such dictates were largely ignored by the first printers, who were not scriveners or language scholars but primarily merchants (dare I say this?) interested chiefly in the commercial success that printing promised: cheaper, faster book production meant more sales and higher profits. (But no scorn, please. If it weren't for merchants like these and their ancestors, what use would a printing press be?)

In the case of William Caxton, who set up the first English press in 1476, the indifference to established standards was due in large part to his extensive traveling as a merchant. His own spelling habits and standards reflected the outdated system he had been taught as a child, infused with myriad foreign influences. In addition, as no one in England was yet familiar with this newfangled machine, he had to hire foreign compositors to work it, and these men were even less acquainted with the current trends of the English language than Caxton himself.

But as more presses were established, printers gradually took up the role that scribes had previously occupied, and they began to realize that it made commercial sense to conform to the style of the day. After all, the book-buying public, which had been increasing exponentially, was aware of which trends were preferred and which were not, and they wouldn't buy books that reflected naïve or outdated understandings of the current standards. (But it took almost five hundred years for them to require dazzling dust-covers.) Still, progress was slow because not all of the book-buyers were so discerning, nor were all of the printers. So there existed simultaneously, for a time, printing houses that produced the cheapest possible books, with little regard for quality or consistency, as well as houses that worked to uphold standards of the scribal tradition. (Hmm, so what's changed?)

The first known use of paper in England was in 1309, and during the period of almost two centuries that followed, it was imported in increasing quantity and began to replace parchment as the material of choice for manuscripts. (You might want to know that parchment was actually the skin of a sheep or goat that was prepared for writing or painting; vellum was an especially fine parchment made from the skin of a calf or a lamb or a baby goat. Then again, maybe you would have preferred *not* to know.) The introduction of paper allowed for an increase in book production that made private reading (as opposed to public recitation) possible for the first time.

This development, combined with the founding of universities and an increased wealth in the merchant class, created an unprecedented demand for books—a demand that was eventually answered by the widespread use of the printing press. Donald Scragg portrays the introduction of paper as a landmark democratization and secularization of literacy: "In earlier centuries, while parchment was expensive and wax tablets were cumbersome, the church easily retained control of education and writing, but with the introduction of paper, mass literacy became both feasible and desirable. In the fifteenth century, private reading began to replace public recitation, and the resultant demand for books led, during that century, to the development of the printing press." Clearly, the press could not have had the success it did—and the resulting effect on spelling—without the introduction of a cheap, but durable surface on which to print. When a paper mill was finally established in England by John Tate in 1495, the cost of printing was significantly reduced, which facilitated the rise in literacy and language standards even more.

Throughout this time of gradual standardization in printed material, private writing remained inconsistent, which is interesting because one might assume that people who cared about the standards of the books they bought would use the same standards in their own private discourse, but this was not necessarily the case.

A possible explanation for such a discrepancy between public and private writing is that the two were considered independent entities, governed by different customs. Printed matter, as public property, was a shared experience—something all readers of books had in common—and as such, had to live up to its role as a communal document. Private writing had only to live up to the shared standards of writer and reader and was allowed to be affected by personal choice and expression. (But who knows? Bad spelling of one's chosen standard may have been rampant. And why not? Things were even worse then than they are now.) While the public/private distinction certainly existed before printing, with professionally copied manuscripts ruling the public realm, the presses widened the rift as the clean, uniform appearance of the printed type gave a more permanent and official look to published works.

But then the distinction began to be blurred by the same technology that had sharpened it. Gradually, the ubiquity of printed material and the ensuing rise in literacy caused the standards for public discourse to be adopted into that of the private realm. And eventually, the cohesion of public and private standards for writing and spelling was helped along by the invention of the personal "writing machine," which first appeared in the early 1700s but did not take on a practical form nor the name "typewriter" until the late 1800s. The typewriter made it possible for private writing to have a uniform, printed look, and in doing so, upped the standard for personal correspondence. Adherence of personal behavior to public standards was very much in vogue at the time of the typewriter's introduction, so it fit right in with popular sentiment. The typewriter's successor in this capacity—the personal computer—perfected the ability of private writing to resemble published text. With the arrival of more and more sophisticated word-processing and page-layout programs, suddenly anyone with the money to buy the right equipment and software could be a "publisher." This evened out appearances—superficial appearances at least—making it harder to discern between "professional" and "amateur" writing, and it also raised the bar for how all written material should look.

A similar effect happened specifically for spelling as a

result of the introduction of the computer spell-check program. Uta Frith describes this effect in her foreword to the *Handbook of Spelling*: "Fortunately, the word processor revolution has liberated the poor speller, but it has also raised expectations of written work to a new level of perfection. Spelling continues to be of concern to teachers, and now *everyone* is expected to have a good command of written language. With spell checkers, the pedantic speller can no longer take unwarranted pride in his achievements, and the poor speller is spared much pain." But while it is true that the spell-checker has, to some extent, made it harder to tell the good spellers from the not-so-good, it is by no means an equalizer. The fact is that for even the most sophisticated spell-checking programs, you must spell most of the word correctly in order to generate any reasonable suggestions. In other words, the modern adage, "Garbage In, Garbage Out" still applies.

Translating an incorrect spelling into a correct one is actually quite a complicated task, requiring many different types of knowledge. Mitton points out that while it is a challenge for both brain and machine, the nature of the challenge differs for each: To correct someone's spelling errors, you must be able to guess what words the person meant, and you must be able to spell them correctly. People usually find the first part easy but the second part harder. "For computers, it's the other way around. Producing a correct spelling is easy—they can store a complete dictionary and retrieve any word as required—the hard part is deciding which word was intended." This statement points out the interdependent nature of our relationship with the spell-checker: it fills in where we fail, and we fill in where it fails. This makes it a convenient tool, but like any other tool, it's how we use it that counts. The spell-checker can be used as a crutch, in which case it is a hindrance to learning, or it can be used as an aid to improvement: it depends on whether the user takes a passive or active role in the process. But to take a truly active role in the use of a tool and to make the best use of what it has to offer, you must understand how it works. Here, then, is a brief explanation of the basic processes at work in the average spell-checking program:

The most basic function of the spell-checker—and the easiest for the computer to perform—is comparing each word on the page to the set of words included in its dictionary. If the word matches one in its list, it's correct; if not, it's incorrect. Of course, there are obvious problems with this method. Ordinary electronic spell-checkers don't contain the equivalent of the *Oxford English Dictionary*—which comprises about 250,000 words (not counting their multiple forms)—so at some point, the program will encounter a word that is unfamiliar, and although it may be spelled correctly, it's flagged as incorrect. Another problem is the variety of forms one word can take through the use of different tenses or the addition of prefixes and suffixes. The ideal electronic dictionary would have to store all these possible permutations as well. With plenty of storage capacity, a spell-checker can contain a good portion of the words and word-forms needed, but better methods have been devised. While most spell-checkers do employ extensive dictionaries, they also employ tables of information about the smaller units that make up a word. This way, the program can check each individual element of a word and its interaction with every other element, and if the pattern doesn't match any known configuration, it can suggest the configurations that the unknown word closely resembles.

The best spell-checkers mimic, in a simplistic way, the spelling processes of the human brain: they have at their disposal several different routes for spelling a word, which can either work independently or interact with each other to produce the desired information. One such route accesses a lexicon, or dictionary, of known words and checks each word on the page against it; another stores information about all the possible relationships between each phoneme (the basic sounds in the language) and grapheme (letters and letter-combinations that represent one phoneme each) in the language, so that words misspelled in a phonetically plausible way (the most common type of spelling error) don't just get rejected by the checker completely but instead produce a list of words that correspond to that phonetic representation.

Another route used in the brain, which has yet to be successfully approximated by a computer and represents one of the biggest challenges to spell-checkers, is the use of context to distinguish between homonyms (words that sound the same, but are spelled differently). The poem at the beginning of this chapter is an example of this problem; all the mistakes it contains are what spell-checker developers call "real-word" errors. The spelling of the word is correct, but it's the wrong word for the context. In a sense, the knowledge required to solve this problem goes beyond spelling into the realm of grammar. Nevertheless, it comes across as a spelling problem in the text and must be addressed by computer spell-checkers if they are ever to approximate the abilities of the best human spellers.

Q & A WITH ROGER MITTON

Roger Mitton is the author of *English Spelling and the Computer*.

MvS: *In your 1996 book,* English Spelling and the Computer, *you stated that the biggest challenges for computer spell-checkers of the time were phonetically misspelled words (such as "shud" for "should" or "youz" for "use") and real-word errors (such as "herd" for "heard" or "plane" for "plain"). Do you think the current technology adequately addresses these problems?*

RM: There has been some slight improvement with the first, but almost none with the second.

MvS: *Is there any cutting-edge technology that you feel might be a real threat to spelling ability and standards?*

RM: It is unclear to me whether the widespread use of spell-checkers will have a good, bad, or neutral effect on people's spelling ability. Another technology that could be influential is speech recognition. If this became very good and widely used, it could reduce the amount of writing that people did, and this could affect their memory for spellings, but this is pure speculation. Anyway I do not accept the implication in the word "threat" that a decline in spelling ability would necessarily be a bad thing. People's ability to do long division by hand has probably declined because of the use of calculators, and I am not upset about that. If technology lightens the burden which many people find spelling to be, or removes the necessity for it altogether, that seems to me a positive development, not a negative one.

Spell-checkers have been around since the 1960s and have been in popular use since the 1980s, so at the turn of the millennium, there are high school students who have never written a paper without the help of a spell-checking program. (Imagine the looks of their essay tests in college.) Does the existence and popularity of the spell-checker mean that future generations will be worse spellers? Maybe. Relying on spell-checkers could dull our "spelling senses" if we don't use them responsibly. It's up to us to make them a teaching tool instead of a crutch. The difference is in the level of awareness we bring to their use. Checking a document mindlessly and letting the program correct every misspelling without taking note of which words we've misspelled—and in what way—will ensure that our spelling never improves and likely cause our ability to decline. But stopping to take note of our problem words and committing the proper spellings to memory can turn a good speller into an excellent one.

The popularization of the Internet has in some ways continued the process of homogenization begun by the arrival of the typewriter and accelerated by the personal computer: it has blurred the public/private and professional/amateur boundaries of writing even further. But this time, instead of raising the standards of personal communication, it has lowered them, at least in the case of e-mail, which, perhaps due to its immediacy, has been regarded by the majority of its users as a medium exempt from the usual structural formalities. In its early years, the Internet was often compared to the "Wild West" because of its generally lawless nature. But as it has grown older, it has become more regulated, inspiring a whole new set of laws and standards, which seems to suggest that e-mail will someday be governed by expectations that are at least analogous to those of traditional correspondence. Certain parallels can be drawn between the Internet's gradual normalization and that of the printing press, which arrived centuries earlier. In both cases, a radical new medium of communication was introduced, which promised a speed and reach that was previously unheard-of, and in both cases, the people introducing these new technologies were outside the professional mainstream of language and communication. In fact, it was partially this outsider status that enabled them to see the potential of the new medium without worrying too much about who was actually minding the store.

If any emergent technology can be perceived as a serious threat to spelling standards and ability, it is speech-recognition, or "talk-to-type," software, which eliminates the author's need to type—and spell—altogether, by converting spoken words directly to text. Speech-recognition technology and its counterpart of sorts, speech-synthesis—which allows the user to listen to words on a page instead of reading them—offer the less-literate and illiterate members of society ways of writing and reading that don't require writing and reading skills. As such, this technology may pose a serious threat to literacy. Currently, a strong motivating force urging illiterate adults to become literate is the desire to avoid the embarrassment of relying on other people to read and write for them. But the more available the talk-to-type and "type-to-talk" technologies become, the less need there will be for illiterate people to learn to read; instead, they'll be able to hide behind their software. Does this mean speech-recognition and speech-synthesis software should be discouraged? No. It can provide an invaluable service to those who otherwise would be incapable of writing or reading printed text. But, as with the spell-checker, there is potential for damage to the skills of the population.

While we do need to be careful about how we use these new technologies, we need not wonder whether automated writing and reading will replace the traditional forms altogether—new technologies rarely replace what came before. A more likely outcome is that several methods will exist side by side, each being used in a different capacity. After all, typing may have taken over for handwriting in certain areas, but it hasn't replaced it by any means; instead, it has merely redefined its purpose. Even if talk-typing did somehow replace traditional typing, the language would continue to change, as it has from the beginning, and the software would continue to be dependent on human beings with excellent language abilities for staying abreast of the changes.

While the ways in which computers have been used to make writing easier and faster have had mixed results with regard to spelling, there are other applications that have been of value to our understanding of spelling. These innovations have already increased our knowledge of everything from the structure of English spelling to the nature of its presence and use in the brain, and they continue to help us discover ways of making spelling easier for children to learn and improving our own spelling, at any age.

The earliest application of computers to spelling research was in storing and analyzing error data—lists of spelling errors generated by hundreds or thousands of test subjects—which are then used to determine different classifications of error and to calculate which types are more frequent than others. Before computers, such data collection and analysis was tedious, time-consuming work. But the use of more and more sophisticated database programs has enabled scientists to spend less time recording and analyzing the data and more time applying it to their particular fields of study. Error information is used in many different disciplines concerned with spelling: linguists use it to understand better the structure of the language and how it evolves over time, psycholinguists use it to test theories concerning the psychological processes involved in spelling, and neurolinguists use it to compare the errors of brain-damaged and healthy subjects to understand better how and where spelling processes are accomplished in the brain. There is also an area of psychological research particularly concerned with applying this information to education in order to learn more about what types of errors can be expected to occur during normal spelling development and what types may indicate developmental problems.

The arrival of personal computers was an important development for spelling education. For example, the "friendly" interactivity of the first Macintoshes enabled teachers to make spelling instruction fun for students, which decreased the stress of performance anxiety, helped motivation and attention, and sped up the learning process. One of the early Mac programs geared toward spelling improvement was a program in which the student was encouraged to make up his or her own mnemonic "rules" for problem words and could hear words on the screen "spoken" by a speech-synthesis mechanism. Chris Sterling, in his "Conclusions" chapter of *Psychology, Spelling and Education,* explains the importance of such computer-oriented education: "Interactive systems, in which the child communicates with the computer, provide the child with guidance but also allow him or her to be actively involved in the learning process. It is the next best thing to individual attention from a teacher."

One of the primary functions of the field of psycholinguistics is to come up with "models" of spelling, which are theoretical representations of the cognitive processes involved in spelling tasks. Originally, these models were described in words. Then mathematical structures were developed to represent them, but there was always a fear that the theory was too far removed from the reality because the simplification inherent in the descriptive process was getting in the way. It was thought that these models perhaps described certain processes in terms we could understand but didn't actually simulate them in an accurate way because they were oversimplified. The advantage offered by computers has been the ability to process the large amounts of data available and produce complex calculations based on that data to form not just representations, but simulations of spelling processes. Gordon Brown and Richard Loosemore, in their contribution to the *Handbook of Spelling* entitled "Computational Approaches to Normal and Impaired Spelling," explain the need for computer models using the following comparison: "In the case of weather forecasting or the modeling of traffic flows, for example, the systems under study are so complex that it is impossible to predict their behaviour without simulating the system in some way. We believe it is likely that this will also turn out to be the case in psychology for models of spelling."

The desire in the field of psycholinguistics to create realistic "maps" of spelling cognition is similar to (and has some procedural crossover with) the aim of those scientists in the field of neurolinguistics who are using artificial-intelligence technology to create computer-generated "neural networks" that simulate language-related activity in the brain. These are computer programs using mathematical representations of neurons that are supposed to

behave in much the same way that real neurons do and
thus can be used to "act out" certain types of brain activity.
Well, maybe. But maybe not, in my opinion. Not everyone
in the neurolinguistic field is confident of the future value
of these computer models, as Loraine Obler and Kris
Gjerlow, in *Language and the Brain*, point out: "Others of us
suspect that, while computers may indeed be able to simulate how brains operate once we know how they do, the
likelihood that brains operate like computers is low. For
one, computers . . . regularly incorporate efficiency as a
governing assumption, whereas it is in the human's interest for brains to have redundant systems set up in case
brain damage of one sort or another comes along." Still,
more and more sophisticated applications of artificial
intelligence are being developed with this concern in mind
and may eventually be able to simulate even the redundant nature of the human brain. But not for a long time.

In the meantime, other technologies are taking up the
task of mapping language in the brain where computer
models leave off. Various sophisticated imaging techniques—such as CAT-scans (Computerized Axial Tomography), PET-scans (Positron Emission Tomography), and
MRIs (Magnetic Resonance Imaging)—are being used to
"x-ray" the brain and help locate specific areas of language
activity. The PET-scan, for example, can be used to monitor
the glucose uptake that occurs when an area of the brain
needs more oxygen for strenuous activity, thereby providing information about the actual location and movement
of that activity. Another, more economical imaging
method is the use of electrodes on the scalp to record the
location of electrical activity in the brain when the subject
responds to certain stimulus. This method is commonly
called ERP, for "event-related evoked potential." As Obler
and Gjerlow explain, "The 'event' is the stimulus; the
evoked potential is the electrical response in the brain that

can be read through the scalp." They go on to describe another procedure, called fMRIs, or "functional MRIs," which, "like cartoons . . . provide a series of snapshots of brain activity so quickly that we appear to see a continuous process unfold on the video screen."

These computer-modeling and imaging techniques are only the latest in a long line of increasingly sophisticated attempts to use technology to help us explain and understand the language and our relationship to it, and they may help us not only to remedy language dysfunction in the disabled or damaged brain but to pinpoint and circumvent the obstacles that exist in healthy brains as well. Clearly, the future looks bright for the relationship between spelling and technology, and that bodes well for more than the future of language: it bodes well for the countless aspects of our lives that language touches.

PART TWO

The METHOD

CHAPTER **6**

THE SECRETS OF
GOOD SPELLERS

My spelling is Wobbly. It's good spelling but it
Wobbles, and the letters get in the wrong places.
                                        —A. A. Milne,
                                        British author

While some of us might not want to admit it, we've
all experienced some "Wobbling" in our spelling at one
time or another. (And in my heart of hearts, I have a lin-
gering fear that you'll find one in this book.) In fact, as
even the best spellers know, it's almost impossible not to
wobble now and then, given the complexity of our lan-

guage. To memorize the spelling of every single word would be a superhuman feat to say the least, not to mention a monumental waste of time and energy, because the best spelling depends on not memorization but simple vigilance—staying aware as you write, then checking your work when you're finished. But for this awareness to pay off, you have to know what to watch out for, and that takes some preparation. So this chapter and the next are designed to provide as thorough a preparation as you can get. Chapter Six offers an explanation of the basic concepts behind effective spelling improvement, and Chapter Seven encourages the practical application of those concepts through quick, effective, and surprisingly painless exercises. (Whoever said, "No pain, no gain," knew nothing about good restaurants.)

Now that we have software that "spells for us" (see Chapter Five to find out how ineffective most spell-checkers actually are), and we'll soon have software that "writes" and "reads" for us too, why is it still important to improve our spelling? Because no technology can make up for a lack of basic skill; you can't live your life hiding behind your spell-checker. And because the poor spelling that stems from that lack is limiting, it closes doors that might otherwise be open. Specifically, it impedes the flow of communication, as Hayden Mead describes in his book *Spelling Made Simple*: "Poor spelling detracts from potentially good writing by distracting the reader, obscuring otherwise clear ideas and masking the intelligence of the writer." Here is how Francis Griffith sees it in the introduction to his book *A Pocket Guide to Correct Spelling*: "A misspelled word . . . may create a negative impression of the writer's general competence or ability to pay attention to details. The result is somewhat like the effect of a gravy stain on the necktie of an otherwise well-groomed man." Errors in written work limit your opportunities. They cause lower grades in school and negative feedback on the job and—perhaps worst of all—can keep you from getting a job in the first place. I myself automatically discard any employment application that contains a spelling error. If an applicant can't even be bothered to check something so basic, how could I trust him or her to oversee anything more important? (Would *you* trust an applicant who graduated from New York University and writes that his favorite book is *Look Homeward, Angle* by NYU English instructor Thomas Clayton Wolfe?)

But even when errors are temporarily hidden—usually with the help of a computer or another person—the quieter, less tangible effects of poor spelling are still there. Insecurity in spelling can cause insecurity in other aspects of writing and in other modes of communication as well because it undermines the self-trust that is essential for confident, effective expression. Since most poor spellers are aware of their problem, they shy away from opportunities to write, hoping to hide their weakness. And when they must write, they limit the words they use to those they feel confident of spelling correctly, thereby unwittingly giving the impression of a smaller vocabulary. My editor at W. W. Norton and dear friend Bob Weil (who is an excellent speller, himself) knows an attorney who doesn't use the word "neighbor" or "friend," not because he doesn't have any—okay, so I'm anticipating your "lawyer" jokes here—but because he's always uncomfortable trying to spell them. Poor spelling can cause otherwise capable people to hold themselves back, and this is unfortunate, not only because of the negative professional, educational, and social effects, but also because it is usually preventable and remediable.

Of course, prevention is easier. As we all know, it's far easier to avoid gaining too much weight than it is to lose it after it's already there. But like losing weight, any adult can still improve his or her spelling, regardless of how good (or how bad) it is. (And you won't even be told you need to exercise!) Even the most challenging tasks often can be solved by breaking them down into more manageable pieces, then working through them in a systematic way. But before attacking a problem, it helps to know what causes it to seem so challenging. So, what is it about English spelling that is so daunting? In a word: irregularity. For one thing, the spelling of many words differs exasperatingly from the pronunciation of them because while the spellings were stabilized centuries ago, the pronunciations continued to change. Then, the sound-symbol relationship is further complicated by the fact that our borrowed alphabet, originally designed for writing Latin, is deficient in representing certain sounds but overabundant in representing others. For example, we have only one letter *e* although there are numerous ways to pronounce it, but we have two letters to represent the same "s" sound (*s* and *c*) and several letters to represent the same "k" sound (*c*, *k*, and sometimes *q*). And then, the influx of many different languages over the centuries has left us with a bevy of possible letter combinations for representing a single sound—most notably, the "ay" sound, which can be spelled *a-y* or *e-i-g-h* or *e-y* or *e-i* or *e-t* or *e-h* or . . . well, you get the idea.

There is no one precept, or even set of precepts, by which all words can be spelled. Instead, there are sets and subsets of "rules," each with its own large collection of exceptions. While there are many consistencies in our spelling system—for instance, the "s" sound is usually written with one *s* at the beginning of a word and with two *ss* at the end of a word, and the letter *q* is almost always followed by the letter *u*—they are not immediately apparent nor universal to all letters, sounds, or words. It's no wonder many of us are confounded by the sight of our spelling system—it appears, at first glance, to make no sense at all! This nonsensical appearance is the product of a turbulent history (a full explanation is in Chapter Four): each culture and age that has come into contact with English has changed it. This has had the good effect of enriching the language immeasurably and making it much more useful for expression but also the not-so-good effect of complicating it woefully and making it much harder to master. Anyone who becomes proficient in English as a second language deserves much more credit than Americans are usually willing to offer. In fact, we often take it for granted.

And the language continues to change today. As Claudia Sorsby puts it, in her book *Spelling 101*, "English speakers are cheerful magpies, good-natured thieves who are constantly adding to the messy nest of language." That "messy nest" is what causes pain for poor spellers and pride for good ones because, as with any difficult task, the mastery of English spelling carries great rewards. In her book *Guide to Better English Spelling*, Edna L. Furness writes, "To a surprising degree, spelling proficiency has become a status symbol. . . . This high status of spelling is mainly due to the many phonetic irregularities in our language. On the other hand, little or no status is attached to spelling achievement in phonetically regular languages such as Spanish and Italian, where a person can spell almost any word he can pronounce." Any vacationer to Italy rapidly learns how to pronounce the names of all the different flavors of gelati. Aside from their taste, now you know why!

It has been argued that the importance placed on spelling, particularly in job-placement settings, is unfair because the rewards for accomplishment and the punishments for deficiency are so severe. On one hand, it may be objectionable that prevailing opinion links spelling—a learnable skill—with inherent qualities such as intelligence and personality, but on the other hand, this situation can be advantageous: that is, a little spelling improvement can go a long way. And if good spelling is all that keeps you from crossing the line between average and excellent in someone else's eyes (not to mention your own), why not give it a try? Beyond that, imagine the benefits of mastery.

A common excuse for not attempting to become a better speller is the argument that you "just can't spell" or that you aren't "a spelling person." (People use the same excuses for poor math skills: "I just can't do math" or "I'm not a math person.") Happily, research has shown that spelling is not an innate aptitude but a learned skill, like any other, which can be affected both positively and negatively by the way in which it is learned and practiced. (See Chapter Two for more information.) Knowing that good—and bad—spellers are made, not born, is the first important step toward spelling improvement because it allows us to take control of this aspect of language in a way that we may not have fully realized was possible.

Another important thing to remember is that many spelling errors are the result of bad or nonexistent proofreading. Surprisingly, we actually know how to spell many of the words we misspell: the problem occurs when either a lack of confidence causes alternate spellings to be considered—and the wrong one is chosen—or the image of the word in the mind does not translate correctly to the page because of an untrained or confused "motor memory" (more on motor memory later in this chapter). If these errors are not caught and corrected in the proofreading stage, they have the same look as errors stemming from a lack of knowledge about the word. So simply adopting more rigorous proofreading habits can eliminate many mistakes. As Sorsby points out, "No one knows how to spell every word, but everyone is capable of checking their work."

But good proofreading does take practice. A study conducted by Harry H. Crosby and Robert W. Emery, and cited in their book *Better Spelling in 30 Minutes a Day,* revealed that spotting misspellings in a paragraph appears to be much more challenging than spelling words correctly that are read aloud, like in routine classroom spelling tests. "In a series of studies using three spelling tests with exactly the same words in them, we learned that if we dictated the words, the average score was about 90 percent. When we put the words in tests . . . we learned that the average dropped to 80 percent. When, misspelling the same words, we put them in a paragraph, we learned that the average dropped to about 60 percent. . . . We deduced that an important part of learning how to spell is to learn how to proofread. . . ."

Something else worth knowing is that despite the chaotic appearance of our spelling system, most of the words we use on a regular basis follow some very learnable patterns. Furness writes, "Research in linguistics has shown that the English language is more phonetic than we realize (approximately eighty-five percent) and that a number of spelling patterns are predictable." Improving your ability to recognize these patterns in more commonplace words is an enormous help in dealing with the less common, more difficult words we encounter. Also, realizing how few words we actually use from day to day—and how few of those actually cause us any spelling problems—makes the task of spelling improvement seem much smaller. The results of a study conducted by Edward L. Thorndike and Irving Lorge revealed that 80 percent of the words we use are drawn from the same set of 1,000 basic, relatively regular words. Harry Shaw's comment on these findings in his book *Spell It Right!* is the following: "If only one thousand different words appear in some 80 percent of all the expressions that one says, hears, writes, and reads, it follows that the task of learning to spell that small number should be simple."

So, just how should you go about the task of improving your spelling? First and foremost, you must diagnose your problem. Like anything else, your spelling can't be fixed until you know what's "broken." Zeroing in on the specific areas that need work will help you not only to focus on the specific types of improvement you need instead of wasting time on areas you've already mastered but also to establish a connection with your problem words.

Your spelling problem (or spelling imperfection) may have a number of different causes: carelessness in writing, reading, listening, or pronunciation; confusion about similar words that are spelled differently; misunderstanding of word meanings in context; or mistakes with suffixes, hyphens, or apostrophes. Understanding the reason you misspell certain words is a giant step on the road to spelling them correctly. And giving words personal significance is the best way to lock them into memory—after all, you don't misspell your own name or the names of close family members, do you? That's because those names are more meaningful words—they have established powerful connections in your mind.

Also, most problems shrink in size upon closer inspection because they become more defined. Trying to ignore a problem is just about the worst thing you can do. It will quietly grow to monumental proportions in your mind as it looms behind you, casting a shadow over all you do. And spelling problems can create a lot of day-to-day anxiety, especially in the workplace. But when they're faced head-on, they soon seem much less threatening. Harry Shaw describes it this way: "When driving a car haven't you often noticed in the distance a hill which looked very steep, the road up it almost vertical? As you got closer, the road seemed to smooth out, didn't it? What seemed an impossibly sharp climb became a simple grade. Learning to spell involves climbing a grade, but not a very steep one, once you get close to the problem."

To get close to your own spelling problems, you'll need to take two diagnostic tests: one to determine which types of spelling errors you most commonly make when writing (for example, do you have the most trouble with endings of words? unstressed syllables? words with double letters?); and one to determine how good your proofreading skills are, and which types of errors you're most likely to overlook when proofreading. Sample diagnostic tests can be found in Chapter Seven.

Once you've identified the classification of your errors, it'll be time to construct a list of your own personal spelling "demons": the words that you almost always misspell and have likely plagued you all your life. (Even top spellers are consistently annoyed by the same words time after time after time.) One encouraging note about this list: it's almost guaranteed that you will be pleasantly surprised by how few problem words you actually have, especially compared to how many you spell correctly all the time. See Chapter Seven for specific instructions on compiling your list. And as you bravely face your mistakes, remember these words from the physicist Niels Bohr: "An expert is a man who has made all the mistakes which can be made, in a very narrow field." You'll be on your way to becoming an expert.

And if you've made previous attempts at spelling improvement but feel that they've been failures, remember: it wasn't you who failed, it was the attempt. You most likely just chose the wrong mode of attack. That's normal. There isn't only one right way to learn. (And for every right way, there are a multitude of wrong ways.) Each of our senses provides a different pathway for learning, and each person's relationship to his or her senses is unique, so hitting upon the right one—or the right combination of several—takes a little experimentation. You may have heard these pathways discussed before: for instance, someone is described as being a "visual learner" or a "hands-on learner." Because we experience the world with all our senses, memories are stored not just as ideas, but as sights, sounds, smells, and tactile sensations as well. So it's a good idea, when attempting to improve your memory and thinking habits, to make use of all your senses. In the beginning, this involves a lot of trial and error; but soon you'll notice that either your visual, aural, or tactile memory is more influential in your learning. (Or just plain makes it easier or more fun.) And there are likely to be combinations. So, because spelling itself does make use of more than one of your senses, it can't hurt to exercise them all.

The parts of our bodies that appear most involved in the act of spelling, and in writing in general, are the hand and the eye. But there's another important participant that we may not notice—the ear. Although English is the least phonetic of all spelling systems, the majority of English words (about 85 percent) actually are spelled the way they sound. So proper pronunciation is an essential part of good spelling. After all, sounding out a word in an effort to spell it won't do you much good unless your sounds are correct. And accurate spelling, in turn, is an essential part of good pronunciation. If your mental image of a word is hazy, errors are bound to creep into your pronunciation. William Proctor illustrates this point in *The Terrible Speller*: "Good spellers are . . . more likely to be adept at proper pronunciation—which is a key element in persuasive speaking. Many times, I've heard otherwise well-educated people say 'grievious' when they mean 'grievous' or 'ek cetera' when they mean 'et cetera.' The reason they make these mistakes is that they don't know how to spell the words!" Remember how everyone laughed when President Jimmy Carter said *nucular* when he meant "nuclear"? And I still haven't forgotten the time a friendly passerby stopped me and said, "Say, are you the one who writes the *Ax Marilyn* column?" Spelling and pronunciation are really two halves of one whole understanding of the sound-symbol relationship, or, as Harry Shefter puts it in *Six Minutes a Day to Perfect Spelling*, "Accurate spelling and proper pronunciation go hand in hand, *and one does wash the other*." The key to improving your spelling through pronunciation is to become better at listening to yourself, which will ultimately help not only your spelling but your speaking as well, easing the discomfort that so many of us feel when talking with others who are judging us.

A good way to improve your pronunciation and by extension, your spelling, is to familiarize yourself with the individual syllables of words: looking up problem words in the dictionary and noting the way the syllables are broken down will help you sound them out correctly because you'll more easily remember each word as a sequence of simple, distinct sounds, instead of one complicated sound. Also, most spelling problems center not just around certain words but around specific syllables within those words, so correct syllabication will really help you pinpoint those problem spots.

One concern related to pronunciation, but which involves the mouth more than the ear, is enunciation: the practice of making articulate sounds. Lazy speech habits—like slurring parts of words together, dropping off the end-sounds of words, and mumbling (which occurs when you lower your voice or close your mouth too much while speaking)—can have as negative an effect on spelling as mispronunciation. This habit starts with the mouth. Eliminating it requires only a slight—but constant, at first—awareness of using more muscle control in your lips and tongue. Your ears will be what you use to test yourself: listen more carefully to both your pronunciation and enunciation when you're speaking.

A common complaint among spellers is that when faced with a correct spelling and an incorrect spelling of the same word, either both versions look wrong or both look right. In each case, the uncertainty stems from the fact that you don't have a clear mental picture of the word. If it's a common word that you misspell frequently, the confusion may stem from the fact that the incorrect version looks so familiar; if it's an uncommon word, you probably haven't seen it in print often enough to have formed a mental picture of it. Also, longer words are harder to remember than shorter words. Shaw describes the process of acquiring visual memories of words in photographic terms: "Simple words like cat, dog, boy and am may be called snapshots—they make an instantaneous clear image on the mind. But words like cataclysm, dogged, boycott and amphibious require longer exposure. That is, you must look at them, probably by syllables, long enough to form clear and precise mental images of them." Shaw's comments bring up an important point about visualizing correct spellings of large words: you'll have much better success and faster progress if you can picture the individual syllables of the word first, then fit them together like pieces in a puzzle.

With practice, you can train your "mind's eye" to

form clear pictures of difficult words in much the same way that you've probably already trained it, albeit unconsciously, to call up an image of your loved ones' faces when you miss them or of a favorite vacation spot when you're feeling stressed. The only difference with word images is that you must add them consciously to your visual repertory. It's not so hard, really. I myself have added the entire dessert menu of my favorite neighborhood coffeehouse to my own memory bank, and I draw upon it often while the movie credits are rolling and I'm waiting for the aisles to clear.

The reason visualization is so helpful is that spelling is primarily a visual activity. Many good spellers depend on visual memory to determine whether a word looks right or wrong. The more finely tuned your visual memory becomes, the better your spelling will be—and the better your observational skills will be, too. You may even find that paying closer attention to the way words look encourages you to notice the world around you more. This is a great side effect because it increases your powers of observation, making you more interested and interesting. It's admirable to be the sort of person that "doesn't miss a thing." Also, better visual control can increase your ability to concentrate, which will help you think better and be more productive.

In addition to hearing and seeing words in greater detail, better spelling requires the ability to feel words more closely—that is, how the shape of a word affects the movement of your hand as you write it. This may sound strange, but memorizing movement is something we do all the time. It's part of what allows us to walk, talk, ride a bike, or play the piano. Sometimes called "muscle memory" or "motor memory," a familiarity with particular sequences of movement is what makes certain activities feel automatic after we've done them many times. We sometimes say of these activities that we could almost do them "in our sleep" because they seem to require no conscious thought to perform. Driving a car is one such activity; signing your name is another. Professional pianists rely on "motor memory" to remember the exact notes so they can concentrate on playing them ever more beautifully.

Just as you can become accustomed to the sight of a misspelled word by misspelling it many times, you can become accustomed to the feeling of writing that word in an incorrect form. It takes time and effort to "unlearn" that memory and replace it with the right one. This applies both to handwriting and to typing on a keyboard: although the two methods of writing involve different kinds of movement, both kinds are learnable. In fact, you probably already have two motor "images" stored for each word you know how to spell—one for handwriting and one for typing.

The key to improving motor memory is not mysterious at all. In fact, it's quite simple: it relies solely on repetition. So writing a word ten times correctly each time you discover that you've written it incorrectly—either through using a spell-checker or a dictionary—is a highly useful (and definitely underrated) method of permanently correcting your spelling of the word. If this sounds tedious, just consider how bothersome it will be to spend your life feeling unsure of yourself every time you come upon a problem word. And consider these words of advice from Epictetus: "Practice yourself, for heaven's sake, in little things; and thence proceed to greater."

Spelling practice that makes use of the senses is probably the best way to correct bad habits and replace them with good ones because it makes you a more experienced speller. But thinking about words—analyzing their structure and becoming more knowledgeable about their meanings and origins—is a great way to become a smarter speller and maybe even a masterful one. These understandings help you build spellings from the ground up, starting from the root of the word and then adding prefixes and suffixes. It can even help you spell words with which you're unfamiliar by teaching you how to combine parts of other words you know to be related or similar.

When spelling improvement is the goal, any activity that causes you to pay closer attention to a word and its structure is a worthwhile one. Many people shy away from the etymological (the study of the origin and history of words, and much more) and other linguistic approaches to spelling improvement because they seem too studious, too much like work. But that's actually not quite right. Those approaches are really just ways of giving words some context—some structure for making sense in your mind. The more you learn, the easier it becomes. Learning about a word's history and origins is like engaging it in a brief conversation: it sheds light on that particular word, makes it clearer in your memory, and also helps you recognize other words that are related to it. This can help you spell whole groups of words correctly, not to mention building your vocabulary.

Take, for example, the Latin root *fin*, which means "boundary." It appears in the words "finish," "finite," "infinite," "define," and "definite"—all words whose meanings are related to the concept of boundary. Once you know the root of a word, you know part of the meaning, and that meaning can then give you a clue to the spelling. "Definite" is a word some people find difficult to spell because of the unstressed syllable in the middle. But if you're familiar with the root *fin* and several of the words that contain it, you should have no trouble figuring out that the unstressed vowel in the middle of "definite" is an *i*.

This method of improvement should be kept light. If you don't enjoy learning about word origins, roots, and meanings, then just look up one or two every now and then, and focus on other methods that you do enjoy. Only techniques that you are willing and able to use will be of any help. But promise yourself that you'll at least give a particular method a sporting try. It can't hurt. And when studying the meanings of words, don't try to memorize the entire dictionary definition; instead, try putting it into your own words or forming a mental image of its meaning. Then, whenever you come across the word in the future, your definition or image will come to mind.

The same light, enjoyable approach should be taken with learning spelling rules. No spelling improvement plan would be complete without some time spent on the study of rules. But it's not necessary (or even wise) to rely on rules to keep your spelling in line. Instead, rules should be regarded more as context. Like the information you acquire from etymology, rules are just another way of familiarizing yourself with words and word types. Also, rules can help simplify matters if you focus on the ones that have no (or very few) exceptions. (For example, instead of trying to remember the spellings of one hundred words, you'll need to remember only the one rule that covers those one hundred words.) For this reason, only the most common rules—rules that apply to large numbers of words and have rare exceptions—are noted in this book.

It's important to adopt a relaxed attitude toward spelling rules: don't let them burden you and discourage you from moving on with your improvement plan. Shaw reminds us that "Words come first, rules second; you should apply a rule, not merely memorize and mouth it." Many of us first learned spelling by rote, which was

the popular method for many years and still has a great
deal of merit. After all, good spelling is based mainly on
good habits, and habits come from repetition. The negative aspect of repetition, though, is the lack of conscious
thought: mindless memorization. It's important to
remain as alert and aware as possible when writing anything from an interoffice memo to the "great American
novel." So it's best to think of rules as groupings or gen-
eralizations that depend on their contents for significance, instead of dictates or mottoes that have value in
and of themselves.

USING THE RULES

If you're the type of person who has trouble "playing
by the rules" (especially when the rules in question have
so many exceptions that they seem hypocritical), whenever you feel yourself resisting, remind yourself that the
words existed long before the rules. These so-called
"rules" are actually more like observations—generaliza-
tions that clever people have devised over the years to
help themselves and others cope with the complexities
of English spelling. The superstar of spelling rules—the
one that everyone has heard at one time or another—is
the following:

> Write *i* before *e*,
> Except after *c*,
> Or when sounded like *a*,
> As in "neighbor" and "weigh."

There's a good reason for this rule's celebrity, beyond
its catchy rhyme: it holds true for over one thousand
words. By learning just one rule, which you've probably
memorized already, you eliminate a thousand words
from your to-do list. Of course, the hard part is remem-

bering which words do not follow this rule, but there's a
suggested rhyme for those, too, which appears in Edna L.
Furness's book. (It may also appear elsewhere.) It doesn't
cover all the exceptions, but it helps with a few troubling ones.

> And except "seize" and "seizure,"
> And also "leisure,"
> "Weird," "height," and "either,"
> "Forfeit" and "neither."

Probably the best approach to this rule (and any
spelling rule) is to use it whenever you're in doubt—
because chances are good that it will work; then, look up
any words that still look wrong. If the words fit the rule,
great. You won't have to wonder about them any more.
If they don't fit, add them to your problem-word list and
learn them by any of the other means mentioned in this
book. And we all know one spelling rule that has virtually no exceptions: follow *q* with *u*.

Beginnings of Words

Here are a few rules to help you form the beginnings
of words:

1. The spelling of a word never changes when a prefix
is added. For example, to add the prefix *dis–* to the word
"satisfied," there's no need to omit an *s*—simply add the
prefix, and you're finished: "dissatisfied" is the result.
The same goes for "unnecessary." To simplify the
spelling of that word, think of the root word "necessary," then add *un–* to the beginning. This rule has no
exceptions, but in order to make the most of it, it helps
to familiarize yourself with the most common prefixes
and their meanings. A list of the prefixes that appear
most often in misspelled words can be found in the next
chapter.

2. A surefire way to know when to use the prefix *for–* instead of *fore–* is to know the meanings of both, which are quite different. *For–* means "not," "against," or "away"; *fore–* means "before" or "in front." Consider words in which the two prefixes appear: *For–* can be seen in "forbid," "forsake," and "forlorn"; *fore–* appears in "forehead," "foresee," and "foreshadow."

3. Meaning also helps to distinguish between the two similar prefixes *inter–* and *intra–*. *Inter–* means "between," and *intra–* means "within." Two words that help demonstrate the difference are "interstate," which means "between states," and "intrastate," meaning "within a state." Being able to distinguish between the two will help make both your spelling and your speech more intelligent.

Endings of Words

Perhaps because so many of the inconsistencies in English spelling happen at the ends of words, there are more rules to help navigate endings than beginnings. Most of them have so many exceptions that they aren't much help, but here they are, anyway:

1. The "final consonant" rule doesn't have an easy rhyme to remember it by, but it holds true for over three thousand words, so it's worth the few minutes it takes to learn. The best way to understand its purpose is to see it in action. Take a look at this list of words, all using the same root word *prefer*: "preferable," "preference," "preferred," "preferring." Why, if these all share the same root word, do two of them double the final consonant before the suffix and two leave the final consonant singular?

The answer lies in the location of the stressed syllable. The first two words, "preferable" and "preference," both have stress on the first syllable—meaning that when they are spoken aloud, they are pronounced PREFerable and PREFerence. The last two, "preferred" and "preferring," have the stress on the second syllable (the last syllable of the root word)—meaning that they are pronounced preFERRED and preFERRing. The location of the stress determines whether that final consonant should be doubled or not: if the last syllable of the root word is stressed, double the final consonant; if not, don't. Note: For this rule to work, the root word must have a single final consonant and a single preceding vowel, and the suffix to be added must start with a vowel. Here are a few more examples: Adding the suffix –*ed* to "omit" makes "omitted." The stress in the new word is in the last syllable of the root word, so the *t* is doubled. Adding the suffix –*ence* to "infer" makes "inference." The stress in the new word is not in the last syllable of the root word, so the *r* is not doubled. Adding the suffix –*ing* to "begin" makes "beginning." The stress in the new word is in the last syllable of the root word, so the *n* is doubled.

2. Here's an ending rule that's easy to remember: always use a *k* after a hard *c* when adding a suffix that begins with *e, i,* or *y*. "Picnic" becomes "picnicked" or "picnicking," "frolic" becomes "frolicked" or "frolicking," and "traffic" becomes "trafficked" or "trafficking."

Plurals

One would think that something as simple as transforming a word from the singular form to the plural would be free from complications, and for the majority of nouns, it is—just add *s*! But there are a few categories of words that differ. Fortunately, they are few enough that learning them is not too taxing:

1. Nouns ending in *ch, s, sh, ss, x,* and *z* add –*es* to form the plural. Examples: "beach/beaches," "crash/crashes," "loss/losses."

2. Most nouns ending in *f* or *fe* switch to *ve* before adding *s* to form the plural. Examples: "loaf/loaves," "knife/knives."

3. Most nouns ending in an *o* preceded by a consonant add *–es* to form the plural. Examples: "potato/potatoes," "hero/heroes." (By contrast, nouns ending in double *o*s, and *o*s preceded by vowels follow the general rule of just adding *s*.)

4. Most nouns ending in *y* preceded by a consonant change the *y* to *i* and add *–es*. Examples: "berry/berries," "city/cities." (By contrast, nouns ending in *y* preceded by a vowel follow the general rule of just adding *s*.)

5. A category of plurals not covered by the above are the words that retain the plural forms of their original language, such as the Latin word "datum" (which we seldom see in singular form; its plural "data" is much more familiar), the French word "tableau" (which adds *x* to form the plural), and words that have completely irregular plural forms, such as "foot/feet," "goose/geese," and "tooth/teeth."

6. There is, by some accounts, one additional way to form the plural that is the cause of some confusion and, as such, has become a subject of debate among style manuals. The debate is concerning whether it is still necessary or appropriate to use an apostrophe to form the plural for letters and figures, as in, "I have three a's and two b's in my name." The position of *The Chicago Manual of Style* is that the apostrophe is unnecessary— italics being sufficient for setting off the letter in question from the *s* that follows it—except in certain proverbial expressions, such as "Mind your p's and q's." This use of the apostrophe was originally meant to avoid confusion—for example, *a's* and *as* would look identical without the apostrophe—but it seems to have caused more confusion than it has avoided, albeit confusion of

another sort. The rules regarding apostrophe use are troublesome for many people to begin with because they involve contraction and possession and have several exceptions. Adding the possibility of using the apostrophe to form the plural opens up another avenue for error that might otherwise be avoided. So the trend now is toward eschewing the use of the apostrophe in this limited plural form. The preferable way to set off letters and numbers without using the apostrophe, made increasingly accessible by the word processor, is through the use of italic type. For example: "I have three *a*s and two *b*s in my name." But style manuals still differ on this topic.

Apostrophes

Proper apostrophe use is an important part of good spelling despite the fact that it involves "only" punctuation because a misplaced apostrophe can lend your writing the same uneducated look as a misplaced letter. And the rules governing the use of apostrophes really aren't as complicated as they might seem, especially if we disregard the debate concerning their use in forming certain plurals and instead focus on the two main categories: contraction and possession.

First of all, it is important to understand the difference between contraction and possession. In his book *Spelling Made Simple*, Stephen V. Ross states, "In contractions the apostrophe is used to show a *mechanical* relationship between words and letters. But in possessives the apostrophe is used to show a *grammatical* relationship between ideas."

Contractions—shortened versions of words or phrases formed through the omission of one or more letters—are created in a straightforward way: the apostrophe is placed where the letters are missing. For example, the contraction of "I am" is "I'm," the apostrophe indicating the spot where the space and the *a* were extracted. The same is true for most other contractions, such as "cannot/can't," "have not/haven't," and "they are/they're." The only exceptions occur for words that would be hard to pronounce as contractions, such as the contraction of "will not" which would be "willn't" if contracted in the usual way, but because that would be hard to say, it has mutated into the irregular form "won't."

Possessives—nouns to which have been added an apostrophe and *s*, or an apostrophe alone, in order to show possession of an object in a sentence—seem straightforward because each one uses an apostrophe, and almost always uses an *s*, but looks can be deceiving. Incorrect use of the possessive form is one of the more common spelling mistakes. So it's important to learn the subtle distinctions between different types of possessives:

Apostrophes are used to show possession in two ways: alone or preceding the letter *s*.

1. To show possession for nouns not ending in *s*, add *'s* to the end. For example: "dog's bone," "rainbow's end," "horse's mouth."

2. For certain nouns ending in *s*, a new syllable is formed by pronouncing the possessive. For these nouns, add *'s* to form the possessive. For example: "boss's daughter," "bus's schedule," "dress's hem." This holds true for proper nouns ending in *s*, as well: "Ross's hat," "Thomas's poetry," "Dickens's novels."

3. To show possession for nouns ending in *s* where pronunciation of the possessive does not add a new syllable, add only an apostrophe to the end. For example: "ladies' clothing," "doctors' fees," "boys' toys."

4. Certain words ending in sibilant (hissing, as with *s* and *z*) sounds take only the apostrophe at the end to form the plural, such as "conscience": "for conscience' sake." This is because of the way it is pronounced. It is

more awkward to say conscience's than conscience'—
hence the different rule regarding this word and others
like it. Ancient proper names, such as Jesus, Moses, and
Euripedes, fall into this category ("Jesus' name," "Moses'
leadership," "Eurpides' plays"). By contrast, a word like
"suitcase," which does end in a sibilant sound but does
not sound awkward with the extra syllable ("suitcase's"),
receives an *'s*.

5. The most common mistake concerning apostrophes is confusing "its," the possessive form of "it," with
"it's," the contraction of "it is." A good way to remember
which is which is to remember the rule for all possessive
pronouns: they take no apostrophe because they have
their own special possessive form, requiring no help
from punctuation: "hers," "his," "ours," and "its" are the
possessive forms of "her," "him," "us," and "it." An even
easier way to remember: don't use "it's" unless you mean
"it is." When you check your written documents, question every instance of "it's," mentally substituting "it is."
If it makes sense, it's right. If not, it's wrong and should
be changed to "its" instead.

6. "Your" (the possessive form of "you") and "you're"
(a contraction of "you are") present the same problem
but don't tend to be confused as often. Nonetheless, all
four words fall into a category called homophones:
words that sound alike but are spelled differently and
have different meanings. Homophones present a different sort of obstacle to spelling from irregular or nonphonetic words because even when they're spelled correctly,
they can betray ignorance on the part of the writer if
they're used in the wrong context. And since a correctly
spelled word that is used incorrectly is often invisible to
electronic spell-checkers, homophone-related mistakes
can be easily missed without good visual proofreading
(that is, the human eye). The best way to avoid problems

with homophones is to become familiar with their definitions. This actually makes them some of the easiest spelling problems to overcome, as there are no rules or tricks to remember. All that's required is adding them to your vocabulary.

AVOIDING CONFUSION

Here are some commonly confused homophones, used in sentences to help clarify their meanings:

1. Capital/Capitol
   If your campaign doesn't succeed, you may end up only vacationing in the capital instead of legislating in the capitol
2. Complement/Compliment
   Your compliment may be the perfect complement to someone's day.
3. Palate/Palette
   If you hold the wrong end of the paintbrush in your mouth, your palate may end up looking like a palette.
4. Principal/Principle
   The clergyman's principles were of principal importance to him.
5. To/Too/Two
   If you've already been to many parks, two more parks may be two parks too many.

Another group of words that are not technically homophones, yet sound alike enough to be readily confused, cause many spelling errors as well:

1. Affect/Effect
   Drinking and smoking affect your health, but a good diet and exercise effect health.

2. Allude/Elude

   Say what you mean and your audience will understand—allude to it and your meaning may elude
   them.

3. Aural/Oral

   If you don't sit still while the doctor examines you,
   your oral examination may become an aural examination.

4. Bazaar/Bizarre

   If you lose your way in a strange city, your trip to
   the bazaar may be more like a trip to the bizarre.

5. Emigrate/Immigrate

   You can't emigrate from one country without
   immigrating into another. Unless, of course, you're
   leaving the planet to colonize the moon.

6. Eminent/Imminent

   If your success is imminent, you may soon be eminent.

7. Farther/Further

   If you leave your home town to go to college,
   you'll be going farther to study further.

A great way to arm oneself against the vagaries of
English spelling is to learn how many possible spellings
there are for each sound. This sounds like a large task,
but there are actually fewer permutations than you
might think, and it's not necessary to memorize them:
simply becoming familiar with them will help to limit
your options when you're unsure of a particular spelling,
thereby speeding up the process of elimination. Edna L.
Furness stresses the importance of learning at least the
most common sound-spelling relationships in order to
be a well-prepared speller: ". . . out of a sampling of
3,000 basic words, 85 percent are spelled with complete
regularity—that is, each sound is spelled with the same

letters in every word every time it occurs. In the unphonetic words, it is rare that more than one letter is irregular. The secret then for the spelling student is to learn
what sounds are always spelled the same way, what
sounds are spelled irregularly, and what the particular
problems behind those irregular sounds are likely to be."

English Sounds and Their Various Spellings

(Uppercase letters indicate a long sound, and lowercase
letters indicate a short sound.)

/A/   a (table), a_e (bake), ai (train), ay (say), ea (break),
     au (gauge), ei (neigh), ey (obey)

/a/   a (flat), au (laughter), al (salve), ai (plaid)

/aw/ aw (saw), au (caught), ou (ought)

/b/   b (ball), bb (bubbly)

/ch/ ch (chest), tch (catch), t (future), c (cello)

/d/   d (door), dd (teddy), ed (walled), ld (could)

/E/   e (me), ee (feet), ea (leap), y (baby), ie (field),
     ei (weird), ey (donkey), eo (people), oe (phoenix),
     i (police), ae (encyclopaedia)

/e/   e (pet), ea (head), ai (said), ay (says), a (many),
     eo (leopard), ei (heifer), ie (friend), ae (aesthetic)

/f/   f (fix), ff (off), ph (phone), gh (laugh), lf (half),
     ft (soften)

/g/   g (gas), gg (gaggle), gh (ghost), gu (guard)

/h/   h (hot), wh (who)

/I/   I (I), ie (pie), i_e (bite), igh (light), y (sky),
     eigh (height), ai (aisle)

/i/   i (sit), y (hymn), ie (sieve), ei (foreign), ai (mountain),
     o (women), u (business), e (England)

/j/   j (jet), dg (judgment), dge (edge), g (gem), ge (age),
     gg (exaggerate), dj (adjust), d (graduate)

/k/   c (cake), k (key), ck (back), cc (account), qu (opaque),
     ch (chaotic), cqu (acquire), cch (saccharine),
     ch (schism), lk (walk), kh (khaki)

/l/ l (lamp), ll (hall)

/m/ m (my), mm (common), mn (solemn), mb (bomb),
     lm (calm), gm (paradigm)

/n/ n (no), kn (knock), nn (sunny), gn (gnome),
     pn (pneumonia), mn (mnemonic)

/ng/ ng (sing), ngue (tongue)

/O/ o (okay), o_e (bone), oa (soap), ow (low), oe (toe),
     ou (soul), ew (sew), eau (bureau)

/o/ o (hot), ou (cough), a (watch), au (caught), aw (saw)

/oi/ oi (soil), oy (toy)

/OO/ oo (boot), u (truth), ue (glue), o_e (move), oe (shoe),
      ui (fruit), ou (through)

/oo/ oo (book), u (put)

/ou/ ou (out), ow (cow), au (sauerkraut)

/p/ p (pie), pp (happy), ph (shepherd)

/kw/ qu (quick)

/r/ r (road), wr (wrong), rr (furry), rh (rhyme)

/s/ s (say), ss (fussy), ci (city), ce (certain), cy (cyst),
     sc (scent), ps (psychology), st (fasten)

/sh/ sh (ship), ti (nation), ci (special), ch (chivalry),
      s (sure), ss (mission), sc (conscience), c (ocean)

/t/ t (time), tt (battle), th (Thomas), pt (receipt),
     bt (doubt), ct (indict), ght (light)

/th/ th (thick, this)

/U/ u (future), u_e (use), ew (few), ue (cue), eu (feud),
     eau (beauty)

/u/ u (thumb), oo (blood), ou (double), a (was), o (son)

/v/ v (voice), vv (savvy), ve (have), f (of), ph (Stephen)

/w/ w (wash), wh (whistle), u (quiet), o (one)

/y/ y (yes), i (onion), j (hallelujah), u (cupid), ew (ewe)

/z/ z (zoo), s (nose), zz (fuzzy), ss (scissors), x (xylophone)

/zh/ s (measure), z (seizure), ge (rouge)

GETTING PERSONAL

I'm an excellent speller. But this doesn't mean that I know how to spell virtually every word. Instead, it means that I virtually never make a spelling mistake. There's a difference. One doesn't make a spelling error unless one doesn't know it. And I nearly always know when I don't know (that is, for sure) how to spell a word correctly. So I look it up first. This behavior is clearly fastidious. *But this behavior is also what makes an excellent speller.*

You don't need to have performed well in spelling bees in order to be a fine speller. After all, how often are you called upon to spell a word aloud? Almost never! Instead, you almost always have the opportunity to write the word down and see how it looks on paper. That's where most spelling errors are caught. Because we're accustomed to reading written words— we don't read *spoken* words—seeing the word often tells us when something's wrong. It will *look* wrong. At this point, stop for a moment. Is there only one obvious place to make a change? If so, make the change and look at the word again. Does it look better? If so, it's probably right now. If not, look it up.

When writing on a computer, disable the spell-checker. Instead, place a question mark in parentheses—like this: (?)—directly following any word you are not *sure* you have spelled right. When you stop writing, go back and look up every one of those words in your electronic dictionary, correcting it yourself and then removing the question mark. This will take only a few seconds for each word. After you finish, *then* run the spell-checker.

When not writing on a computer, look up your question-marked words in an unabridged dictionary and correct them. Then give your writing to a friend or family member who is an excellent speller. Ask him or her to highlight any word that he or she believes is misspelled. Now look up each one of *those*.

Like starting an exercise program, this will be toughest in the beginning. Unlike an exercise program, however, it will get easier and easier until you see almost no mistakes at all. At that point, you will be a good speller for life.

Many of my readers have asked whether I thought it would be helpful to read books about improving one's spelling. I hope so: you're holding such a book in your hands.

The information and exercises in this and the next chapter are designed to present you with a full range of the best options for improvement. You should try them all before deciding which work best for you. Then, personal choice should determine not only which methods to use, but also when, and for how long. Plans that propose to work within a specified amount of time are bound to fit some schedules and temperaments but not others. And we all know how that usually works: it never works for *us*. That's because each of us learns so differently—not everyone enjoys spending fifteen minutes studying spelling during breakfast, but then again, some do. (And it's better than reading about yesterday's train wrecks.) So it's important that you allow yourself a trial period during which you'll discover which approaches are best for you. In the process, you'll get to know yourself a little better, and that's always a good thing. Also, as Bertrand Russell said, "Anything you're good at contributes to happiness."

No matter what kind of speller you are—at least at the moment—you can always benefit from regular practice at being aware as you write. If thinking about spelling as you write is too distracting for you, write first, then proofread afterward. But if you can learn to review as you write, you'll save yourself a lot of time and effort. The best advice is the following: *spell with care*. Spelling carefully includes both being mindful of spelling as you write and conducting a thorough check when you're finished.

In spelling, as in anything else, be kind to yourself: focus on how far you've come instead of on how far you have yet to go. (I'll bet you've improved already.) And relax. If spelling rules frustrate you, concentrate on mastering your problem words in another way. Once you've become an excellent speller, it won't matter what route you took to get there—just that you succeeded.

CHAPTER 7

SOME THINGS TO KEEP UP YOUR SLEEVE

Spelling is a skill that few notice—unless you
make a mistake!   —WILLIAM PROCTOR,
The Terrible Speller

Spelling is a silent skill: it's usually noticed only when
it's wrong. And that fine spelling is taken so completely
for granted is actually a good thing. It means that we
have a solid spelling standard for our language—an
essential asset for any advanced civilization. It also
means, however, that the goals of spelling improvement

are different from those of other skills. Usually when we resolve to improve our performance, we do it to stand out among others, to be better than the rest so that the people we wish to impress (like prospective employers, business associates, and really great dates) will take notice. But with spelling, it's opposite. Because we don't want to call attention to bad spelling, we work at making our spelling so good that it's invisible. It is, in this sense, comparable to the goal of the ballet dancer—a presentation so perfect as to appear effortless.

As good dancers and spellers alike know all too well, a lot of work goes into that final illusion of ease. And it's rewarding work—effort that pays off not only in the area being consciously improved but in related areas as well. Just as ballet practice, in addition to producing a beautiful performance, makes all the dancer's movements more graceful on stage and off, spelling practice strengthens not just spelling but also all the capacities, physical and mental, that it exercises. So training your eye and ear to recognize the visual and aural shapes and patterns of words will improve not only your spelling but your general looking and listening abilities as well. And the truth is that excellent spellers do stand out: they get better grades on papers in school, better jobs, and a special degree of respect from peers for their consistently precise, clear writing.

Also, developing discipline in one area of your life inevitably carries over into others. Once you've reached the point at which spelling awareness and practice is a habit, you're likely to discover that you're being more observant and systematic in other ways as well. So there's nothing to be lost—and everything to be gained—by practicing your spelling. This chapter offers specific ways of putting into practice the ideas discussed in the previous chapter. While Chapter Six laid the crucial groundwork for spelling improvement, providing you with information about the best methods and why they work, the activities, exercises, and tricks presented in this chapter are the means for putting that knowledge to work.

So once you've decided to improve your spelling, how do you begin? With a little self-examination. Before you can patch the holes in your spelling knowledge, you must locate them. Start by writing down all the words that you know you consistently have trouble spelling. (Look them up first, and write them down correctly, of course.) It may be hard to come up with these at first, but it's the first step toward creating your personal list of spelling "demons," as they're sometimes called—words that are, for whatever reason, especially hard for you to spell. It's a good idea to start this list somewhere permanent, like a notebook you buy for this purpose. And if you start the list toward the back of the notebook and do exercises and activities in the front, you'll have a complete, self-contained record of your progress, good for periodically checking back on your accomplishments and congratulating yourself on how far you've come.

You should try to have the notebook at your side whenever you need to write anything, whether it's an office memo, school paper, or letter to a friend, because problem words are bound to occur to you as you write, and keeping the notebook handy will allow you to add them to your list when they're still fresh in your mind. Keep a dictionary handy as well, so you can record the words correctly. You don't need to complete the list before starting your improvement plan—instead, just start with the most obvious words and keep adding words as you go along.

DIAGNOSTIC TESTS: NO. 1

Once you've written down all the problem words that occur to you at the moment, take the following diagnostic test. This will help you to see which types of spelling errors you make most often and direct you to those areas of improvement that need the most attention. As you work your way through the questions, more problem words may come to mind. If this happens, be sure to stop and add them to your list.

What's missing? Or is the word correct as shown? Note your answers on a piece of paper.

1. "By persist____ntly remaining single, a man converts himself into a permanent temptation. Men should be more careful." —Oscar Wilde

2. "The writer who neglects punctuation, or mispunctuates, is liable to be misunderstood. . . . For the want of merely a comma, it often o____curs that an axiom appears a paradox, or that a sarcasm is converted into a sermonoid." —Edgar Allan Poe

3. "The stars are the apexes of what triangles! I just looked up at a fine twinkling star and thought that a voyager whom I know, now many day____ sail from this coast, might possibly be looking up at that same star with me." —Henry David Thoreau

4. "There are i____numerable questions to which the inquisitive mind can in this state receive no answer."—Samuel Johnson

5. "By the time a child is eight or nine, he has developed a passion for his own music that is even stronger than his passions for procrastination and w____rd clothes." —Bill Cosby

6. "Mirth is better th____n fun, and happiness is better th____n mirth." —William Blake

7. "Every society honors it___s live conformists and it___s dead troublemakers."   —Mignon McLaughlin

8. "It has been an unchallengeable American doctrine that cranberry sauce, a pink goo with overtones of sugared tomat___s, is a delectable necessity of the Thanksgiving board and that turkey is uneatable without it... There are some things in every country that you must be born to endure. . . ."   —Alistair Cooke

9. "We are respons___ble for actions performed in response to circumstances for which we are not respons___ble."

—Allen Massie

10. "Talent is an amalgam of high sensitivity; easy vulnerability; high sensory equip___ment (seeing, hearing, touching, smelling, tasting—*intensely*); a vivid imagination as well as a grip on reality; the desire to communicate one's own experience and sensations, to make one's self heard and seen."   —Uta Hagen

11. "Radio news is bear___ble. This is due to the fact that while the news is being broadcast the disc jockey is not allowed to talk."   —Fran Lebowitz

12. "Any plan conc___ved in moderation must fail when the circumstances are set in extremes."   —Prince Metternich

13. "It is always easier to fight for one's princip___s than to live up to them."   —Alfred Adler

14. "You___ an expatriate. You've lost touch with the soil. You get precious. . . . You hang around in cafés."

—Ernest Hemingway

15. "The progress of freedom depends more upon the maintenten___nce of peace, the spread of commerce, and the diffusion of education, than upon the labors of cabinets and foreign offices."   —Richard Cobden

16. "Nothing in the world was i___relevant: the stars on a general's sleeve, the stockmarket quotations, the olive harvest . . . Nothing."   —Jean Genet

17. "The f___rther one goes, the less one knows."   —Lao-Tzu

18. "Ideas are powerful things . . . They dictate where a man must concentrate his vision. . . . . They provide him with all___s and make him enemies."   —Midge Dector

19. "For me, the cinema is not a slice of life, but a p___ce of cake."   —Alfred Hitchcock

20. "There is nothing which at once ___ffects a man so much and so little as his own death."   —Samuel Butler

21. "Great writers arrive among us like new diseases—threatening, powerful, impatient for patients to pick up their virus, irresist___ble."   —Craig Raine

22. "Of course we women gossip on occasion. But our appetite for it is not as avid as a man's. It is in the boy___ gyms, the college fraternity houses, the club locker rooms, the paneled offices of business that gossip reaches its luxuriant flower."   —Phyllis McGinley

23. "Money itself isn't lost or made. It's simply transfe___red from one perception to another."   —Oliver Stone

24. " 'One *can't* bel___ve impossible things.' 'I daresay you haven't had much practice,' said the Queen. 'When I was your age, I always did it for half-an-hour a day. Why, sometimes I've bel___ved as many as six impossible things before breakfast.' "   —Lewis Carroll; Alice and the White Queen in *Through the Looking Glass*

25. "Nothing is more dangerous than a friend without discretion; even a prudent enemy is prefer___ble." —Jean de la Fontaine

26. "Inanimate objects are classified scientifically into three major categor___s—those that don't work, those that break down and those that get lost."   —Russell Baker

27. "To find a form that a___co___modates the mess, that is the task of the artist now."   —Samuel Beckett

28. "Hero___s are created by popular demand, sometimes out of the scantiest materials."   —Gerald W. Johnson

Now check your answers against those listed at the end of this chapter, noting the ones you got wrong on a piece of paper. The answers are grouped into seven categories: Prefixes, Final Consonants, Plurals, Apostrophes, *Ie/ei,* Unstressed Vowels, and Homophones. When you're finished checking your answers, you'll be able to see which types of errors you most commonly make, and so, which areas need the most improvement. Now that you have an idea of what your problem areas are, you'll be more aware of words that belong to those categories as you come across them. But even if you believe that your difficulties lie in only one area, that doesn't mean that you should skip practice in other areas; it simply means that you may need to spend more time on the activities that strengthen your weakest "spelling muscles."

DIAGNOSTIC TESTS: NO. 2

There's one more self-test you'll want to do because, although you now have some idea of the specific types of trouble you have when you're writing words, you may not know how good you are at reading over your own work and spotting the errors nor what sorts of errors you're most likely to overlook. This is important because thorough proofreading is an essential part of good spelling. Read through the following paragraph, jotting down in your notebook the numbers of the misspelled words as you spot them.

Its (1) finaly (2) that (3) time (4) again (5)—time (6) to (7) anounce (8) the (9) winner's (10) of (11) this (12) years (13) essaye (14) contest. (15) We (16) were (17) priveleged (18) enough (19) to (20) receive (21) allmost (22) fourty (23) fascinaiting (24) entrys, (25) and (26) nearley (27) all (28) of (29) them (30) were (31) concerning (32) personel (33) experiances. (34) It (35) ocurred (36) too (37) the (38) judges (39) that (40) perhapes (41) their (42) is (43) truth (44) to (45) the (46) old (47) addage: (48) "Great (49) minds (50) think (51) allike." (52) But (53) whatever (54) the (55) reason (56) for (57) the (58) repition (59) in (60) themes, (61) the (62) fact (63) remaines (64) that (65) each (66) indavidual (67) made (68) it (69) his (70) or (71) her (72) owne. (73)

Now check your list of misspellings with the one at the end of the chapter. How did you do? Is catching errors in a paragraph easier for you than preventing them while you write, or is it more challenging? Either way, you should now have a clearer picture of your strong and weak points. Together, these factors make up your unique spelling profile. You are now ready to start working on that profile, methodically smoothing over the rough spots and polishing your overall technique.

THE VALUE OF A DICTIONARY

A little-known fact about good spellers is that they have a silent partner constantly at their sides, helping them out when the going gets tough. That quiet companion is a dictionary. Is this cheating? No, it's *learning*. Good spellers are independent spellers, but this doesn't mean that they can't get help from a dictionary. On the contrary, most use one frequently, and their independent spelling gets better each time they do.

The most important thing to remember regarding the dictionary is to keep it within reach when you write. Maybe you think there's not much difference between having the dictionary at arm's length and having it in the bookcase down the hall, but it's an important point, and there is a difference—you need to feel that it's immediately available to you. For example, if you're sitting in bed late at night writing a letter and feel unsure of the spelling of a word, are you more likely to get up and take the dictionary from a bookshelf in another room or just change to a synonym that you feel confident about spelling? Most of us—myself included—would opt for the latter. But this is a missed opportunity for improvement. Had the dictionary been sitting faithfully within your reach, you would have been able to use your first-choice word instead of opting for the runner-up.

One of the obstacles keeping poor spellers from using their dictionaries is the occasional annoyance of not being able to find the word they're looking for. This is a valid concern, but mainly if most of your spelling problems center around the beginnings of words. Still, there's a solution, one that helps you not only to find the word but also to improve your overall spelling ability in the process: familiarize yourself with all the possible spellings for particular sounds. For instance, if you're looking up "pneumonia," you may look under *n* because it starts with an *n* sound. If you don't find the word under *n*, and you know of a few other possible spellings for that sound, you can continue your search instead of giving up in frustration. And having success at this method is positive reinforcement—you discover the spelling of a word through your own active effort, and the feeling of *eureka!* will help cement the correct spelling in your mind. The next time you'd like to use the word, you may either find it in a flash or not even need to look it up at all. A list of sounds and their various spellings can be found in the previous chapter.

Another way you can use dictionaries to improve your spelling is by paying attention to the way the entries are separated into syllables. This can help divide the problem word into more-easily-retrievable pieces in your memory so that the next time you need the word, you won't have to pull it out all at once; instead, you can try building it from the smaller pieces that compose it. (Champion spellers do this routinely.) The syllable division also can help you recognize certain common prefixes, suffixes, and roots so that when you need to spell related words, you can remember the spelling of the familiar piece of the word and go from there. To get an idea of how common certain prefixes are, the next time you look up a word, glance up and down the page at the words that surround it. Because the entries are listed alphabetically, you can see all the words that begin with a particular prefix together.

The primary function of a dictionary, of course, is to provide the meanings of words, and this aspect, too, can be used as a tool for spelling improvement because the stronger an association you form with a particular word, the more likely you are to remember its spelling. Having a clear idea of the meaning of a word will prompt you to make it part of your everyday vocabulary—meaning that group of words you know you can depend on yourself to use and spell correctly. After the definition, a good dictionary will note the origin of the word, and this too can help with spelling because each word of origin often has several modern cousins and learning the spelling of one word that sprang from that root will help you spell other related words correctly. Also, glancing at the words surrounding the one you looked up may remind you of other words you have difficulty spelling so that they can be added to the list of problem words in your notebook.

Dictionaries are good for pronunciation practice too because each entry always includes a phonetic representation of the word. Using this pronunciation guide to say the word aloud correctly will not only give you an auditory link to the spelling of the word—so that saying it to yourself the next time you need to spell it will help you remember the spelling—but also ensure that you're pronouncing it correctly so when you do sound it out in the future, you don't get foiled by your own mispronunciation.

As you read in the last chapter, proper pronunciation is an important part of correct spelling. Here's another good way to practice and improve your pronunciation: Using your list of problem words, look up each one in the dictionary, then say the word aloud while looking at the pronunciation guide to make sure you're doing it correctly. Then say the word while looking at the correct spelling. Pronounce each syllable distinctly, even stopping between syllables to make it easier to enunciate each sound clearly. Try to make a conscious connection in your mind between the sounds you're making and the correctly spelled word on the page.

THE VALUE OF LISTENING

Pronunciation practice is most effective when you're paying close attention to how you sound, and because we're all so used to hearing ourselves talk, it's hard to really listen to ourselves—that is, to notice the subtle differences between the ways we pronounce words and the ways they're pronounced by other people. The remedy for this is making your voice sound a little different from the way you're used to hearing it. One way to do this is by recording your voice on a tape recorder and playing it back. But be forewarned: many people don't like the way they sound on tape, partly because the voice is unfamiliar. (It's also partly because our voices are flattered by our own acoustics, but try not to think about that!) This strangeness, if you can endure it, is exactly the kind of exercise that helps you pay attention to your pronunciation. Listen to yourself say the words from your problem list. Are you pronouncing them the way they appear in the dictionary? Are you mispronouncing any words in the same way that you misspell them, perhaps by adding a letter that isn't supposed to be there or subtracting one that should be?

If you prefer not to listen to yourself on tape, there are other ways of making your voice sound different. Just cupping your hands over your ears will make your voice sound deeper and more resonant, and this change alone may help you to pay closer attention. You can even practice your pronunciation in the shower because, as anyone who sings in the shower knows, the acoustics in most bathrooms lend an almost operatic quality to your voice. So now you have a legitimate excuse to belt it out in the shower—you're improving your pronunciation and enunciation.

THE VALUE OF VISUALIZING

In addition to listening to words more closely and familiarizing yourself with the way they sound, paying close attention to the way words look can be an important aid to improving your spelling. To demonstrate the importance of visualization, close your eyes and think of a word you have no trouble spelling, like your own name. Picture it in your mind as if you were looking at it on a giant neon sign. You should be able to make out each individual letter. Now think of a word that you know is difficult for you to spell, and picture it with your eyes closed. You may be able to see the letters at the beginning of the word, but the end might look a little blurry, or you might find yourself waffling between two letters at a certain place in the word, so that first an *e* appears, then an *a*. If it's a really tough word, your mental picture might look like a broken sign over an old drugstore with some of the letters missing completely. With enough time spent looking at that problem word—studying its beginning, middle, and end, and getting to know the placement of each individual letter—you can fix that broken sign so that it's as clear and bright as the one upon which you imagined your name emblazoned.

Try focusing on problem spots. For example, the problem spot in "weird" is the *e-i* pair. To make those letters the dominant feature in the word instead of the area that loses clarity when you try to picture it in your mind, type the word in lowercase letters except for the trouble spot, which you should type in uppercase letters, like this: wEIrd. Stare at the word for a few seconds, and practice displaying it on that neon sign in your mind. Now you've made the problem spot the focal point of the word—which it should be, anyway, because it's causing all the trouble. Give it the attention it deserves, and the next time you picture the word before writing it down, you may see those bold capital letters.

Most large words contain smaller words within them. To become more aware of the internal patterns of words, look at the longer words in your problem list. How many smaller words can you find in each of them? "Paradigm" is a tricky word to spell because of its silent *g*, but if you notice that the word *dig* is nestled inside it, you may have an easier time remembering the *g* the next time you write it.

THE VALUE OF MOTOR MEMORY

How many things can you do with your hands without actually looking at them or even thinking much about what they're doing? Most people can sign their names while their eyes and minds are otherwise engaged, and anyone who plays an instrument will tell you that the easier pieces almost seem to play themselves. Good typists can watch the words appear on the screen and think about the next sentence without a glance or a thought to their fingers tapping away at the keyboard. What allows us to accomplish these amazing feats is motor memory: when we do something often enough, our bodies "remember" the patterns of sensations so well that we can do it without thinking. Motor memory can be a great help in spelling, but it can hurt your spelling if the version of a word you're accustomed to writing is incorrect. So it's important to focus on those words that you have a habit of writing incorrectly—especially if you always write them in exactly the same incorrect way—and retrain your "spelling muscles" to spell them correctly.

This retraining can be accomplished through simple repetition: whenever you come across a misspelled word in your writing, you should correct your mistake and then write the word correctly several times by hand (a few times in cursive and a few times in print) and type it correctly several times on the keyboard so that no matter which way you write the word in the future, all will be better trained for the correct spelling. Familiarizing your hand with the "feel" of words also helps increase your general awareness of their structure so that you're more likely to catch misspellings when you're proofreading.

COMMON ROOTS

It's important to remember that the best spellers don't simply memorize every word. Memorization techniques usually are best left to the unusual or irregular words (granted, there are a lot of them in English) and words that, for whatever reason, you just can't seem to keep straight. For those words that share attributes with many others, it's much more efficient to learn the root, then build any number of words from there. Below is a list of the most common word roots along with their meanings. Familiarizing yourself with just one root will help you spell the whole group of words that share that root, so it's well worth the time you spend. In addition to helping your spelling, knowledge of word roots will also expand your vocabulary.

ROOT	MEANING	EXAMPLE
anim	mind, life	animal, animate, unanimous
arch	rule, govern	anarchy, archives, archetype
auto	self	autobiography, autonomy, automatic
cap, cip, cept	take, hold	capable, anticipate, accept
ced, cess	go, yield	proceed, recede, access, success
dic, dict	say, speak	dictate, contradict, dedicate
fac, fact	do, make, act	facsimile, faction, perfect

ferr, fer	carry, bring	ferry, infer, refer, fertile
gen, gener	class, kind	gender, general
grad, gress	walk, go, step	graduate, progress
log	word, speak	logic, eulogy, psychology
medi	middle	medieval, mediate, medium
mit, miss, mise	send, throw	transmit, emit, submission, surmise
port	carry	portable, export, important
sed, sess	sit	sedentary, session
spec, spect	look, see, appear	speculate, spectacle, conspicuous
string, strict, strain	bind, draw tight	stringent, restrict, restrain
ten, tin, tain	hold	tenure, pertinent, maintain
vers, vert	turn	adverse, invert
voc, vok	call	vocalize, evoke

COMMON PREFIXES

But recognizing roots is just one valuable piece of the puzzle of words. To really excel at word-building, it's important to know the most common prefixes and suffixes as well. To add to your knowledge, study these lists of the most valuable ones to know.

PREFIX	MEANING	EXAMPLE
a–	not	amoral, asymmetrical
ad–	to, against	adjunct, adverb
ambi–	around, both	ambiguous, ambidextrous
ante–	before	antechamber, anteroom
anti–	opposite	antisocial, antibiotic
auto–	self, same	autograph, autobiography
bio–	life	biography, biology
com–	in association	combine, compare
de–	away, down	demerit, degrade
dis–	apart, not	disability, disagreement

extra–	beyond, without	extraordinary, extrasensory
hyper–	far beyond	hyperactive, hypertension
il–	not	illogical, illegitimate
im–	opposed	immoral, imbalance
inter–	among, between	interchange, interact
intra–	within	intramural, intravenous
ir–	not	irresponsible, irreconcilable
mono–	one, alone	monopoly, monologue
post–	behind, after	postscript, postpone
syn–	together, with	synthetic, syndrome
tel– (tele–)	distant	television, telephone
trans–	across, beyond	transcend, transmit
un–	not, reverse of	unfair, unnoticed

COMMON SUFFIXES

Abstract noun suffixes, signifying "state of," "act of," or "quality of":

SUFFIX	EXAMPLE
–al	committal, approval
–age	marriage, salvage
–ance (–ence)	performance, convergence
–tion (–ion, –sion)	proclamation, union, recession
–dom	kingdom, freedom
–hood	childhood, falsehood
–ice	cowardice, avarice
–ism	plagiarism, communism
–ment	government, agreement
–ness	happiness, playfulness
–ship	hardship, penmanship
–th	warmth, depth
–ty	maturity, modesty

Concrete noun suffixes, signifying "one who does," or "one who is":

SUFFIX	EXAMPLE
–an (–ant, –ent)	guardian, informant, student
–ard (–art, –ary)	drunkard, braggart, notary
–ee (–eer, –ess)	referee, auctioneer, lioness
–er (–ar, –ier, –or)	caller, scholar, clothier, chancellor
–ic (–ist, –ite,–yte)	cynic, hedonist, luddite, acolyte
–ling	darling, underling

Adjective suffixes, signifying "resembling," "full of," "belonging to," or "degree":

SUFFIX	EXAMPLE
–ac (–al,–an, –ar,–ary)	cardiac, casual, Freudian, planar, customary
–ed	toasted, corrugated
–ful	sorrowful, joyful
–ish	foolish, peevish
–ive	secretive, argumentative
–ory (–ary)	obligatory, cursory, customary
–ous	spacious, courteous
–ward	inward, wayward
–y	happy, greedy

Adjective suffixes, signifying "capable of":

SUFFIX	EXAMPLE
–able	bearable, foreseeable
–ible	incredible, visible
–ile	fertile, infantile
–ive	furtive, cursive

Verb suffixes, signifying "to make":

SUFFIX	EXAMPLE
–ate	procreate, infiltrate
–en	embolden, deepen
–fy	fortify, justify
–ize (–ise)	materialize, advertise

Exercise

Try combining the entries from these lists to form complete words: choose one prefix, one root, and one suffix at random, and see if any or all of them fit together to form a word. This exercise is like flipping through a children's book in which the pages are split horizontally into three parts, allowing the reader to mix and match, for example, a chicken's legs with a dog's torso and a man's head: some combinations produce monsters, but some produce surprisingly cohesive wholes—new combinations that you hadn't expected to work. Chances are that you'll find more successful double combinations (prefix+root or root+suffix) than successful triple combinations (prefix+root+suffix), but triples aren't uncommon. Looking at the examples provided in the lists will help get you started.

Exercise

As you're developing your ability to assemble and dissect words, keep in mind that another important "shape–change" words undergo is the transformation from singular to plural form. The "rules" of pluralization—at least the general patterns that plurals tend to follow for certain groups of words—look complicated and unreliable on paper. But for most practical purposes, all you need to remember is to add an *s* for most words, *–es* for sibilant endings, and *–ies* instead of *y* for *y*–endings. To demonstrate this, try a little plural practice: look at each noun suffix in the above list (the first two groups of suffixes are the noun suffixes) and form the plural of the suffix. You'll see that they all follow the norm, and nearly all of them simply add *s* to form the plural. Nouns ending in *o*s and *f*s and nouns that have completely irregular plural forms, like "child/children" and "foot/feet" are admittedly tricky—and downright weird—but chances are, you've got most (if not all) of those plurals already committed to memory. Those that do give you trouble should be added to your list and given special attention.

Take Note

You may have noticed that none of the words discussed so far use an apostrophe to form the plural. This is because apostrophes are *never* used to form the plural except in the rare case that a letter is used as a word in a sentence (as in, "Mind your p's and q's,") and italics are not available (as in, "Mind your *p*s and *q*s,"). *The Chicago Manual of Style* and many other style manuals frown on even that rare usage because it's so irregular and causes so much confusion for other types of plural formation. It also has been made all but obsolete by the fact that computers and even some typewriters have made italics so accessible.

The apostrophe's two main duties (and according to many, its only duties) are showing possession and contraction, so whenever you're in doubt about whether an apostrophe is needed, ask yourself if the word in question is possessive or a contraction of two words. But keep in mind that there is one specific type of possessive that doesn't take an apostrophe: the personal pronouns ("me/mine," "you/yours," "she/hers," "he/his," "we/ours," "it/its"). Luckily, there is a logical reason for their lack of apostrophes: they each have their own unique possessive form, and so they don't need to use punctuation to indicate possession. Many problems are caused by one personal pronoun in particular: "its." The trouble usually stems from a confusion between the possessive personal pronoun "its" and the contraction of "it is": "it's." The secret to solving that problem is to mentally expand "its" to "it is" whenever you're in doubt. If the sentence still makes sense, the apostrophe should stay. If not, toss it out. Here's an example: In the sentence, "Life has its ups and downs," should "its" have an apostrophe or not? Expand "its" to "it is," and the sentence reads "Life has it is ups and downs." Clearly, the "its" in this phrase is not a contraction and therefore does not need an apostrophe.

THE VALUE OF PROOFREADING

Here's the bad news: no matter how much you improve your ability to spell, you're still going to make some mistakes. But here's the good news: becoming a better proofreader can help you catch them. Spelling doesn't end once you've written the word. You also must read it to be sure it's correct. This is more difficult than it sounds. In fact, paradoxically, the better you are at reading, the worse you may be at proofreading because many good readers are fast readers—they absorb the meaning of a word without spending much time looking at it. And plenty of words can get passed over completely if the reader knows enough from the surrounding words to infer the ones he or she is skipping. But this habit makes for bad proofreading.

It's important to understand the difference between reading and proofreading. Most reading is like driving through town at 30 miles an hour—you get a good general sense of how the town is laid out and where certain buildings are in relation to others, but you don't absorb all the individual street names or meet any people. By contrast, careful proofreading is like walking through town at a leisurely pace—you can see the cracks on the sidewalk and the expressions on people's faces, and although you don't immediately grasp the overall layout of the streets, eventually, through repeated and varied walkthroughs, you gain a more thorough understanding of the town's structure and character than you could ever have achieved in a car. The best readers and proof-readers find a happy medium between the two: a mixture of speed and attention to detail that might be analogous to exploring the town on a bicycle.

Here are some tips for improving your proofreading: typewrite instead of handwrite whenever possible. The clear, even quality of the type makes errors much more visible. Also, you may be so familiar with your own hand-writing that everything "looks right" at first glance even if it's wrong. Use an electronic spell–checker only after you've checked the document thoroughly yourself, and if it catches any mistakes that you didn't catch, pay special attention to each error before correcting it. Is it a typo, or is it a genuine problem word that should be added to your list? Either way, it's important to spend a few moments noticing exactly what you got wrong and how to correct it. That way, you're much less likely to make the same mistake again, and even if you do make it again, you're more likely to catch it before it's too late. It's important to read for meaning, too, not only for grammatical reasons, but also to catch any misused homophones.

MNEMONIC DEVICES

Let's jump ahead and imagine that you've already spent a significant amount of time and energy improv-ing your spelling, you use the dictionary often, and you're making considerable progress—but there's still a small group of words that just won't stick in your mind no matter what you try. This is where mnemonics come in. Human beings have probably been using mnemonic devices—phrases, songs, words, and ideas that help us to remember things—for as long as we've had things to remember. We can all recall a few that helped us prepare for tests in grade school, and there are countless sayings that people of all ages use to get through life. The ridiculous name, "ROY G BIV," which helps us remember all the colors in the rainbow in order from outside to inside (red, orange, yellow, green, blue, indigo, and violet) is one example, and the phrase, "Spring forward, fall back," which helps us remember how to set our clocks for daylight savings time, is another. Some of us will even refuse to have a phone number that doesn't spell out a memorable word or phrase for fear that we won't remember it!

But despite the proven effectiveness of mnemonic devices, it's clear that they make sense only occasionally. Regarding spelling, especially, it's just not practical to rely on them—and the device is usually longer than the word it helps you remember! But for those few words that resist all other methods, mnemonics may do the trick. The best device is one you devise yourself, and there are several reasons for this: First of all, you're more likely to remember something you created. Second, your own creations are likely to be more useful to you because they'll be tailored to focus on whatever part of the word is most troublesome for you. And third, creating them will force you to pay closer attention to the word and its structure, a good exercise in itself. Mnemonic devices that call attention to words within words are particularly effective because they help you break up the word into smaller, more manageable parts. And don't worry if they sound absurd, because the more absurd they are, the more memorable they'll be.

COMMONLY MISSPELLED WORDS

The most effective method of improving your spelling is also the most straightforward: repetition. The more familiar you become with the correct spelling of a word, the better your spelling of that word will be. Below is a list of five hundred frequently misspelled words. You may find some of your problem words among these, and you may also discover new problem words among those listed. Studying the list may even have the unexpected effect of actually making you feel good about your spelling because the percentage of words on this list that you don't know how to spell is bound to be quite small. Don't feel obligated to practice every word: only practice those that give you trouble.

500 COMMONLY MISSPELLED WORDS

A

abrupt
absence
absorption
abundance
accede
accelerate
acceptable
accessible
accessory
accidentally
accommodate
accompanying
accomplish
accumulate
achievement
acquaintance
acquainted
acquiesce
acquire
across
adjournment
admissible
admittance
advantageous
advertisement
advise
affiliate
against
aggressive
airplane
alignment
allege
almost
allotment

allotted
already
although
altogether
aluminum
amateur
amendment
among
analysis
analyze
anecdote
angel
annual
answer
apostrophe
apparatus
apparent
appearance
appointment
appropriate
architect
arguing
argument
around
arouse
arrangement
article
ascend
asphalt
assignment
assistance
asterisk
athletics
attendance
attorneys

auctioneer
audible
authority
auxiliary

B

bachelor
ballot
bankruptcy
banquet
basically
battery
beginning
behavior
believable
believe
beneficial
benevolence
bicycle
boundary
breathe
brilliant
brochure
budget
bulletin
bureau
business

C

calendar
campaign
canceled
cancellation
candidate
career
careful

carrying
cashier
ceiling
cemetery
census
certain
changeable
character
chief
choose
chose
clientele
collateral
college
colossal
column
coming
commitment
committee
comparatively
competitor
concede
conceivable
conceive
condemn
confident
conscience
conscientious
conscious
consecutively
consistent
conspicuous
continuous
contribute
control

controlling
controversy
convenience
correspondent
criticism
criticize
curiosity
curious
cylinder

D

deceive
decision
defendant
deferred
deficient
deficit
definite
delegate
delinquent
dependent
describe
description
desirability
desirable
despair
desperate
develop
development
diagnosis
different
disappear
disappoint
disbursement
discrepancy
dissatisfied
distinct
divine

dominance

E

ecstasy
efficient
eligible
eliminate
embarrass
eminent
encyclopedia
endorsement
enterprise
envelop
envelope
environment
equipped
erroneous
especially
evidently
exaggerate
exceed
excellent
exhaust
exhibition
existence
exorbitant
experience
explanation
extension
extraordinary

F

facsimile
fallacy
familiar
fascinate
fascinating
feasible

finally
financially
flexible
fluorescent
forcible
foreign
forty
franchise
fulfill
fundamental

G

gauge
genuine
gesture
gigantic
gnawing
gorgeous
government
governor
grammar
gratuity
grocery
grudge
guarantee
guidance

H

handkerchief
handsome
haphazard
harass
heavily
hectic
height
hindrance
homely
homogenize

humorous
hurrying
hygiene

I

illegal
illegible
illiterate
imagine
imitation
immediately
immigrant
inaugurate
incidentally
indelible
independence
indispensable
inflammable
inhabitant
inoculate
installation
integrate
intercede
interest
interfered
interpretation
interrupt
irrelevant
irresistible
irrevocable
issuing

J

jeopardize
jewelry
journey
judgment
justifiable

justified

K

khaki
knowledge

L

labeling
laboratory
lacquer
ledger
legitimate
leisure
liaison
library
license
lightning
likable
liquefy
listen
livelihood
loneliness
luxury

M

magnificent
maintenance
manageable
management
maneuver
manual
manufacturer
manuscript
marriage
mathematics
mediocre
mileage
miniature
miscellaneous

misspelled
modern
morale
mortgage
movable
murmur
mysterious

N

necessary
nickel
niece
nineteenth
ninety
ninth
noticeable
nuisance

O

oblige
occasionally
occurred
occurrence
omission
omitted
oneself
operate
opponent
opportunity
oppose
opposite
optimism

P

pamphlet
parallel
parcel
partial

particular
peaceable
peculiar
perceive
performance
permanent
permissible
perseverance
persistent
personally
personnel
persuade
philosophy
physician
piece
planned
playwright
possession
practical
prairie
precede
preceding
precious
prefer
preferable
preliminary
presumptuous
prevalent
privilege
probably
procedure
proceed
profession
professor
prominent
promissory
pronunciation

propeller
psychology
publicly
pursue
pursuing

Q

quantity

R

realize
receipt
receive
recipient
recommend
reconcile
recurrence
reference
referred
relevant
relief
reminisce
renown
repellent
repetition
replies
restaurant
reveal
rhubarb
rhyme
rhythm
ridiculous
rotary

S

safety
salable
scholastic

scissors
secretary
seize
sensible
separate
shepherd
shining
shipment
siege
significance
similar
simultaneous
since
sincerely
sizable
skeptical
sneak
souvenir
sovereign
specifically
speech
splitting
statistics
strength
strictly
subsidy

substantial
succeed
success
successor
sufficient
summary
suing
superintend-
ent
supersede
surgeon
surprise
survey
susceptible
suspicious
symbol

T

tailor
tangible
tariff
technique
televise
television
temperament
temporary

tenant
tendency
terrible
territory
their
theory
therefore
transferred
triumph
truly
tying
tyranny

U

unanimous
undoubtedly
unique
until
unusual
usable
useful
using

V

vaccinate
vacuum
varies

vegetable
villain
visible
visitor
vitamin
volume

W

waiver
warranty
weather
weird
welfare
whether

X

xylophone

Y

yacht
yield
youth

Z

zealous
zenith
zephyr
zoology

And Just For Fun . . .

WEIRD PRONUNCIATIONS

George Bernard Shaw, the acclaimed playwright and avid proponent of spelling reform, supposedly said that "fish" could also be spelled *ghoti* because *gh* is pronounced like an *f* in "cough," *o* like an *i* in "women," and *ti* like the *sh* in "nation." Of course, *ghoti* isn't likely to become the more popular spelling, but it demonstrates the diversity of sound/symbol relationships in English spelling. Below are more "alternate spellings" for English words. Can you figure out the traditional spellings on which these alternates are based? You can find hints in the list of sounds and spellings in Chapter Six.

1. JAST—If you wish to be agreeable, you may make this your reply.
2. CHAUTH—Many people find a warm one of these to be a comfort.
3. CQUOLD—If you have one of these, you and the goats have something in common.
4. TIUPH—Ice is its worst enemy.
5. TOCCHEOMN—Food for some, an insult to others.
6. WHAIQUTHYCH—An apt description of Monday morning traffic.
7. WROEOEIGHKNED—What you wish you could do after saying the wrong thing.

You can check your answers with those at the end of the chapter.

FUNNY WORD PATTERNS

You can also play with the letter patterns in words and see what surprises turn up. Reversing words can sometimes produce different words, as Marshall McLuhan pointed out when he joked, "'Diaper' backward spells 'repaid.' Think about it." Other examples are: "desserts," whose mirror image spells "stressed;" "deliver," whose "opposite" is "reviled;" and "star," which spells "rats" in the other direction. Sometimes words turn out to be spelled the same way backward and forward—these are called palindromes. Some examples of palindromes are "level," "redder," and "deified." Even entire sentences can be constructed so that they read the same in both directions. For example, the letters contained in this sentence: "A man, a plan, a canal—Panama!" are in the same order both forward and backward. Other sentences like this include, "Madam, I'm Adam," "Was it a bat I saw?" and "Straw? No, too stupid a fad. I put soot on warts."

SERENDIPITOUS ANAGRAMS

Or you can rearrange the letters in words to produce anagrams. Some wordsmiths maintain that the term "anagram" should be reserved for words that are formed from the letters of other words with the same meaning such as "endearment," whose letters can be rearranged to form "tender name," and "H.M.S. Pinafore," which can be "scrambled" to read, "name for ship," but that words formed from the letters of nonsynonymous words should merely be called transpositions. Most dictionaries, including the *Oxford English Dictionary*, do not make this distinction. Regardless of what we call them, though, these pairs of words sharing the same letters can be fun to construct even if they're not actually synonymous. For example, "listen" and "silent" are transposals of one another and seem to have something in common, as do "masher" and "harems" and "angriest" and "tearings."

REVERSING LETTERS

Some words can be changed into other words with only one or two letter reversals. For example, to change "able" to "bale," one need only switch the positions of the *a* and *b*. It can be fun to trace the steps between two words. See if you can fill in the steps between the pairs of words below, reversing the position of two adjoining letters in each step:

Example:

PEST	1. EVIL	2. SPOT	3. DEAR	4. PETALS
PSET	_____	_____	_____	_____
SPET	_____	_____	_____	_____
SPTE	VILE	STOP	_____	_____
STPE			_____	_____
STEP		READ	_____	
				PLATES

Once you've had fun with games like these, you may find yourself becoming more word-savvy in everyday life. You can encourage this trend by doing the crossword puzzle in the newspaper now and then or even seeking out more complicated word games in books and magazines. If you're stuck in traffic or bored silly on public transportation, try looking at the words on signs and billboards and mentally rearranging the letters to form new words or check to see if the words spell different words (or the same words) in reverse. At the most basic level, you'll find that just being more curious about words improves your relationship with them. And whenever you see a word with which you're unfamiliar, take a minute to look it up. You may be surprised by the satisfaction and positive results you can get from this quick, simple activity.

Practice is a state of mind. Think of yourself as practicing not just when you do exercises from this chapter, but all of the time. In other words, whenever you write anything, treat it as a training session, because that's what it is: real-life practice—like a dress rehearsal. The "practice" mindset gets you into the habit of constant improvement. That is, it takes improvement out of the classroom setting and brings it into your life in general. With time, the careful, thorough mindset you've developed will have become a habit. It will be part of how you write.

ANSWERS

Diagnostic Test No. 1

(1) persistently, (2) occurs, (3) days', (4) innumerable, (5) weird, (6) than, (7) its, (8) tomatoes, (9) responsible, (10) equipment, (11) bearable, (12) conceived, (13) principles, (14) you're, (15) maintenance, (16) irrelevant, (17) further, (18) allies, (19) piece, (20) affects, (21) irresistible,

(22) boys', (23) transferred, (24) believe, (25) preferable, (26) categories, (27) accommodates, (28) heroes.

Below, the answers are grouped according to the type of error they address. If you write down the seven error types in your notebook and then tally up the errors under the appropriate headings, you'll see which areas need the most attention.

Apostrophes: (3) days', (7) its, (14) you're, (22) boys'.
Final Consonants: (10) equipment, (15) maintenance, (23) transferred, (25) preferable.
Homophones: (6) than, (13) principles, (17) further, (20) affects.
Ie/ei: (5) weird, (12) conceived, (19) piece, (24) believe.
Plurals: (8) tomatoes, (18) allies, (26) categories, (28) heroes.
Prefixes: (2) occurs, (4) innumerable, (16) irrelevant, (27) accommodates.
Unstressed Vowels: (1) persistently, (9) responsible, (11) bearable, (21) irresistible.

Diagnostic Test No. 2

Here are the numbers of the misspelled words and their correct spellings:
(1) It's, (2) finally, (8) announce, (10) winners, (13) year's, (14) essay, (18) privileged, (22) almost, (23) forty, (24) fascinating, (25) entries, (27) nearly, (33) personal, (34) experiences, (36) occurred, (37) to, (41) perhaps, (42) there, (48) adage, (52) alike, (59) repetition, (64) remains, (67) individual, (73) own.

Weird Pronunciations

1. JAST—YES (The "y" sound is spelled with a j, as in "hallelujah," the "e" sound with an a, as in "many," and the "s" sound with st, as in "fasten.")

2. CHAUTH—CAT (The "c" sound is spelled ch, as in "schism," the "a" sound with au, as in "laughter," and the "t" sound with th, as in "Thomas.")

3. CQUOLD—KID (The "k" sound is spelled cqu, as in "acquire," the "i" sound with an o, as in "women," and the "d" sound with ld, as in "could.")

4. TIUPH—SHIP (The "sh" sound is spelled ti, as in "nation," the "i" sound with a u, as in "business," and the "p" sound with ph, as in "shepherd.")

5. TOCCHEOMN—CHICKEN (The "ch" sound is spelled with a t, as in "future," the "i" sound with an o, as in "women," the "ck" sound with cch, as in "saccharine," the "e" sound with eo, as in "leopard," and the "n" sound with mn, as in "mnemonic.")

6. WHAIQUTHYCH—HECTIC (The "h" sound is spelled wh, as in "who," the "e" sound with ai, as in "said," the "c" sound with qu, as in "opaque," the "t" sound with th, as in "Thomas," the "i" sound with a y, as in "hymn," and the final "c" sound with ch, as in "chaotic.")

7. WROEOEIGHKNED—REWIND (The "r" sound is spelled wr, as in "wrong," the "E" sound with oe, as in "phoenix," the "w" sound with an o, as in "one," the "I" sound with eigh, as in "height," the "n" sound with kn, as in "knock," and the "d" sound with ed, as in "crawled.")

Reversing Letters

1. EVIL	2. SPOT	3. DEAR	4. PETALS
VEIL	SPTO	DERA	PETLAS
VIEL	STPO	EDRA	PELTAS
VILE	STOP	ERDA	PLETAS
		REDA	PLEATS
		READ	PLAETS
			PLATES

APPENDIX

ORGANIZATIONS RELATED TO SPELLING

Scripps Howard National Spelling Bee
PO Box 371541
Pittsburgh, PA 15251-7541
www.spellingbee.com

Sponsors national spelling bees, and promotes the development of local spelling bees in schools. Also offers word lists, activities, study aids, and tips online.

Simplified Spelling Society
13 Hurstleigh Drive
Redhill, RH1 2AA, UK
www.les.aston.ac.uk/sss/

Founded in 1908, the SSS promotes research and debate on ways of reforming English spelling, and attempts to persuade the public, policy-makers, and relevant agencies of the need for and practical possibilities of reform.

Society for the Preservation of English Language and Literature (SPELL)
PO Box 118
Waleska, GA 30183
www.mindspring.com/~spellorg/

Determined to resist the "abuse and misuse" of the English language in the media. Sends "Goof Cards" to perpetrators of incorrect English, sponsors a scholarship-essay competition for high school seniors, and publishes style guides and a newsletter.

American Dialect Society
English Department, MacMurray College
Jacksonville, IL 62650
www.americandialect.org

Founded over a century ago, the ADS is a scholarly association dedicated to the study of the English language in North America. Activities include an online community, annual meetings, during which the official ADS "Word of the Year" is elected (the official word of 1998 was "e-" as in e-mail, e-commerce, etc.), and the publication of a quarterly journal, *American Speech*.

Dictionary Society of North America
University of Wisconsin–Madison
6131 H.C. White Hall, 600 N Park St.
Madison, WI 53706
http://polyglot.lss.wisc.edu/dsna/

Fosters scholarly and professional activities relating to dictionaries. Promotes an exchange of information and ideas among members through meetings, research projects, and publications (newsletters, journals, bibliographies, directories).

American Name Society
English Department, Northern Illinois University
DeKalb, IL 60115
www.wtsn.binghamton.edu/ANS/

Founded in 1951 to promote onomastics—the study of names and naming practices—both in the United States and abroad. Primarily concerned with discovering what really is "in a name," and investigating cultural insights, settlement history, and linguistic characteristics revealed in names. Publishes *NAMES: A Journal of Onomastics*.

Modern Language Association
10 Astor Place
New York, NY 10003-6981
www.mla.org

Promotes the study and teaching of language and literature

through books and journals, annual conventions, job assistance, prizes and awards, and style guidance.

Linguistic Society of America
1325 18th Street NW, Suite 211
Washington, DC 20036-6501
www.lsadc.org

Founded in 1924 for the advancement of the scientific study of language, the LSA provides scholarly meetings, publications, and special activities to advance the discipline. Membership also includes a subscription to the quarterly journal *Language*.

American Literacy Council
680 Fort Washington Avenue
New York, NY 10040
www.under.org/alc/

Provides resources and assistance to persons and organizations who promote literacy in America. Resources include hardware grants, computer software, and publications that promote solutions to the problem of illiteracy.

National Council of Teachers of English
1111 West Kenyon Road
Urbana, IL 61801-1096
www.ncte.org

Dedicated to improving the teaching and learning of English and the language arts at all levels of education. Provides teaching ideas, publications, grants, and job opportunities to elementary, high school, and college instructors. Website offers information relevant to anyone interested in English language standards and use.

WEBSITES RELATED TO SPELLING

www.spellingdoctor.com
Features articles and advice on spelling improvement, and promotes understanding of English spelling.

www.dictionary.com

In addition to its dictionary function, this site features an online community for people interested in words, games, a "word of the day," writing resources, and a forum for asking "Dr. Dictionary" a word question.

www.m-w.com

The Merriam-Webster site features a dictionary, thesaurus, "word of the day," transcripts of a public radio program devoted to language, and an explanation of the process by which new words are allowed entry into the dictionary.

www.oed.com

The Oxford English Dictionary site offers a behind-the-scenes look at the world's most venerated dictionary, as well as arguably the most informative online "word of the day" feature available.

BIBLIOGRAPHY

Brown, Gordon D. A., and Ellis, Nick C., editors. *Handbook of Spelling: Theory, Process and Intervention.* Chichester: John Wiley & Sons, Ltd., 1994.

Brown, James I., and Pearsall, Thomas E. *Better Spelling: Fourteen Steps to Spelling Improvement.* Lexington: D. C. Heath and Company, 1996.

Castley, Anna. *Practical Spelling: The Bad Speller's Guide to Getting It Right Every Time.* New York: Learning Express, 1998.

Chomsky, Noam, and Halle, Morris. *The Sound Pattern of English.* Cambridge: MIT Press, 1991.

Craigie, W. A. *English Spelling: Its Rules and Reasons.* New York: Folcroft Press, 1927.

Eckler, Ross. *Making the Alphabet Dance: Recreational Wordplay.* New York: St. Martin's Press, 1996.

Emery, Robert W., and Crosby, Harry H. *Better Spelling in 30 Minutes a Day.* Franklin Lakes: Career Press, 1995.

Frith, Uta, editor. *Cognitive Processes in Spelling.* London: Academic Press Inc., 1980.

Furness, Edna L. *Guide to Better English Spelling.* Lincolnwood: National Textbook Company, 1996.

Gates, Arthur I. *The Psychology of Reading and Spelling, with Special Reference to Disability.* New York: AMS Press, 1972.

Green, Jonathon. *Chasing the Sun: Dictionary Makers and the Dictionaries They Made.* New York: Henry Holt and Company, 1996.

Griffith, Francis. *A Pocket Guide to Correct Spelling.* New York: Barron's Educational Series, Inc., 1997.

Knowles, Gerry. *A Cultural History of the English Language.* New York: Oxford University Press, 1997.

Landau, Sidney. *Dictionaries: The Art and Craft of Lexicography*. Cambridge: Cambridge University Press, 1989.

Leith, Dick. *A Social History of English*. New York: Routledge, 1997.

Mead, Hayden. *Spelling Made Simple*. New York: The Berkley Publishing Group, 1996.

Mersand, Joseph E.; Griffith, Francis; and Griffith, Kathryn O'D. *Spelling the Easy Way*. Hauppauge: Barron's Educational Series, Inc., 1996.

Mitton, Roger. *English Spelling and the Computer*. New York: Longman Group Limited, 1996.

Obler, Loraine K., and Gjerlow, Kris. *Language and the Brain*. Cambridge: Cambridge University Press, 1999.

Proctor, William. *The Terrible Speller: A Quick and Easy Guide to Enhancing Your Spelling Ability*. New York: William Morrow & Company, 1993.

Rankin, Joan L.; Bruning, Roger H.; and Timme, Vicky L. "The Development of Beliefs About Spelling and Their Relationship to Spelling Performance." *Applied Cognitive Psychology* 8 (3) (June 1994): 213–32.

Ross, Stephen V. *Spelling Made Simple*. New York: Doubleday, 1990.

Russell, David. *Characteristics of Good and Poor Spellers*. New York: AMS Press, 1937.

Scragg, Donald. *A History of English Spelling*. New York: St. Martin's Press, 1975.

Shaw, Harry. *Spell it Right!* New York: HarperPaperbacks, 1994.

Shefter, Harry. *Six Minutes a Day to Perfect Spelling*. New York: Pocket Books, 1976.

Sledd, James, and Ebbitt, Wilma R., editors. *Dictionaries and That Dictionary: A Casebook on the Aims of Lexicographers and the Targets of Reviewers*. Chicago: Scott, Foresman, 1962.

Sorsby, Claudia. *Spelling 101*. New York: The Philip Lief Group, 1996.

Sovik, Nils; Frostad, Per; and Lie, Alfred. "Can Discrepancies Between IQ and Basic Skills Be Explained by Learning Strategies?" *British Journal of Educational Psychology* 64 (3) (Nov. 1994): 389–405.

Stemmer, Brigitte, and Whitaker, Harry A., editors. *Handbook of Neurolinguistics*. San Diego: Academic Press, 1998.

Sterling, Chris M., and Robson, Cliff, editors. *Psychology, Spelling and Education*. Bristol: Longdunn Press, 1992.

Vallins, George Henry. *Spelling*. (Revised by Donald Scragg, with a chapter on American spelling by John W. Clark.) London: A. Deutsch, 1965.

Venezky, Richard. *The American Way of Spelling: The Structures and Origins of American English Orthography*. New York: Guilford Press, 1999.

Venezky, Richard. *The Structure of English Orthography*. The Hague: Mouton, 1970.

Watson, Alice E. *Experimental Studies in the Psychology and Pedagogy of Spelling*. New York: Columbia University Bureau of Publications, 1935.

INDEX

About the Author

Marilyn vos Savant is a national columnist: she writes the "Ask Marilyn" question-and-answer column for *Parade* magazine, the Sunday magazine distributed by 325 newspapers, with a circulation of 37.2 million and a readership of 83 million, the largest in the world. She also has worked as a television news contributor, appearing weekly on the "Ask Marilyn" segment for the evening news on WCBS, the New York affiliate for the CBS network. She spends her spare time writing plays, the first of which was produced in New York City last year.

Ms. vos Savant, who uses her mother's maiden name, is married to Robert Jarvik, M.D., the inventor of the Jarvik 7 artificial heart; they have two grown children, Mary and Denny. She also works for her husband's company, Jarvik Heart, Inc., which manufactures artificial hearts for use during and after surgery. They reside in Manhattan.

Her special interests are in education and humanitarian medicine. She serves on the Board of Directors of the National Council on Economic Education, and she is a member of the Advisory Boards of the National Association for Gifted Children and the National Museum of Women's History. She was named by the members of Toastmasters International as their No. 1 Educational and Social Communicator for 1999.

Ms. vos Savant was listed in the *Guinness Book of World Records* for five years under "Highest I.Q." for both childhood and adult scores and has now been inducted into the Guinness Hall of Fame.